Capital Allocation

The Financials of a New England Textile Mill
1955 – 1985

By: Jacob McDonough

ISBN: 9798631760202

This book contains some direct quotes from the annual reports of Berkshire Hathaway, Blue Chip Stamps, Wesco Financial, and GEICO. This book also contains direct quotes from the Letters to Shareholders written by Warren Buffett and Charlie Munger. These quotes have been printed with the permission of Warren Buffett and Charlie Munger.

Table Of Contents

I.   The Preface   *4*

II.   The Prologue   *7*

III.   The Textile Mill 1955 - 1962   *12*

IV.   The Investment 1962 - 1965   *23*

V.   The Transition 1965 - 1967   *27*

VI.   The Acquisitions 1967 - 1969   *39*

VII.   The Expansion 1970's   *67*

VIII.   The Other Companies   *93*

IX.   The Conglomerate   *137*

X.   The Conclusion   *159*

I. The Preface

> "It is dangerous...to apply to the future inductive arguments based on past experience, unless one can distinguish the broad reasons why past experience was what it was."
> – John Maynard Keynes[1]

Berkshire Hathaway is one of the greatest companies in the history of the world. Much has been written about both Warren Buffett and Berkshire explaining this point. This book is not an attempt to replace or rephrase any of those great works, but instead to supplement them. Readers of this book are encouraged to first read Warren Buffett's Letters to Berkshire Hathaway Shareholders, as well as some of the biographies written about Buffett's life.

When a person is considering making an investment, much time and effort is spent analyzing financial data. However, people often rely on more generalized storytelling to analyze past investments. The goal of this book is to bridge that gap. *Capital Allocation* attempts to analyze Berkshire through the years from the perspective an investor might have had at that point in time.

When preparing for upcoming games, U.S. football teams watch actual game film instead of viewing the SportsCenter highlights on ESPN. History books tend to be more like the highlights, showing the quarterback launching the ball and then the receiver celebrating in the endzone with a creative touchdown dance. This is not a criticism of history books, as generalized storytelling can be very beneficial for a broad audience, especially for those with little expertise in the subject. However, the highlights are of little use to the practitioner who needs to make decisions in the future. A football coach reviews film to see how a lineman picked up a block when a linebacker was blitzing, allowing for enough time for the quarterback to make the throw. A quarterback reviews footage of the defense to see how they adjusted their coverage when a receiver runs a certain route. *Capital Allocation* was written for practitioners who wish to analyze more of the finer details of Berkshire as a company.

While this book isn't for everyone, I felt that more attention should be given to the company's financial statements and annual reports. The goal was to give readers a chance to view some of the important information that Warren Buffett viewed when making operating and investing decisions. This is the book I wish I had while learning about the greatness of Berkshire Hathaway.

I would like to highlight three items to keep in mind when reading this book. First, I am a huge fan of Berkshire and Warren Buffett, and I am sure that this admiration caused me to be biased in some way. Second, hindsight is another bias that this book is sure to suffer from. Hindsight can be blinding as it makes things seem more obvious today than they really were at the time. Events should be judged based on their probabilities not their outcomes, but that can be difficult when the outcome is staring you in the face. I tried to look at each detail with a fresh perspective, but I am sure these biases influenced my writing. Third, every investment opportunity needs to be weighed against all other options available to the investor at that time. The opportunity cost is a crucial part of any investment decision. While I researched Berkshire and some of the companies it invested in, investors during this time period also needed to take into account the opportunity cost of missing out on other options. The decisions to not invest in certain companies might have been more important than the investment decisions Berkshire did make. Other than considering interest rates during the time period, fully incorporating opportunity cost into this book was not feasible.

II. The Prologue

In the 1960's, Warren Buffett invested heavily in a company called Berkshire Hathaway. The business was struggling, and the industry was in the midst of a steady decline. The company had no real competitive advantages to begin with, and would not be able to compete with cheaper labor overseas.

In addition to Berkshire, Buffett also owned a stake in the Diversified Retailing Company as well as a firm called Blue Chip Stamps. Diversified Retailing merged with Berkshire in 1978, and Blue Chip followed suit and merged in 1983. Diversified Retailing was formed by Buffett, Charlie Munger, and Sandy Gottesman to acquire a Baltimore department store called Hochschild Kohn. Blue Chip was a publicly traded company that operated a rewards program with retailers.

Hochschild Kohn went out of business in 1984 after struggling to compete with the rise of discount retailers. Berkshire's textile operations were shut down the following year. Blue Chip saw its trading stamp revenue decline 92.6% from $124.2 million in 1969[1] to $9.2 million in 1982[2]. The Berkshire Hathaway in which Buffett built his fortune basically started with these three failed businesses. Despite these headwinds and missteps, Buffett was able to turn Berkshire Hathaway into one of the most valuable companies in the history of the world.

How could this be possible?

Buffett took control of Berkshire in 1965. The company's market value reached $21.7 million the year before[3]. At the end of 2019, the market value of Berkshire was about $553.5 billion. This means that Berkshire grew to be 2,550,930% or 25,509 times more valuable than when Buffett took over. Berkshire's market value grew at a compound annual growth rate of 20.3% over the 55 year period.

The top ten companies in the 1965 Fortune 500 are listed in the following table[4]. This table is sorted by revenue. Berkshire Hathaway was nowhere close to making it into this list in 1965. Gulf Oil, the 10th ranked company on the list, had revenue that was 64 times higher than Berkshire and profits that were 173 times higher than Berkshire.

1965 Fortune 500	Revenues	Profits
1) General Motors	$16,997,000,000	$1,734,800,000
2) Standard Oil of New Jersey	$10,814,700,000	$1,050,600,000
3) Ford Motor	$9,670,800,000	$505,600,000
4) General Electric	$4,941,400,000	$237,300,000
5) Mobil	$4,499,400,000	$294,200,000
6) Chrysler	$4,287,300,000	$213,800,000
7) U.S. Steel	$4,077,500,000	$236,800,000
8) Texaco	$3,573,800,000	$577,400,000
9) International Business Machines	$3,239,400,000	$431,200,000
10) Gulf Oil	$3,174,300,000	$395,100,000
N/A - Berkshire Hathaway	$49,300,685	$2,279,206

Berkshire ranked 4th by revenue in 2019 in the Fortune 500. The change from 1965 to 2019 was almost unbelievable, especially when you compare them to General Electric (GE), for example. In 1965, GE had what appeared to be an insurmountable lead over Berkshire. GE can trace its roots back to Thomas Edison and the invention of the light bulb, while Berkshire just manufactured textiles. GE had revenues of $4.9 billion and profits of $237.3 million in 1965. Both of these metrics happen to be about 100 times larger than Berkshire, which had $49.3 million of revenues and $2.3 million of profits that year[5]. GE would also be fortunate enough to have Jack Welch as CEO for 20 years starting in 1981. Many consider Welch to be one of the greatest business leaders of all-time. Fortune magazine, for example, named him "Manager of the Century" in 1999. The market value of GE in 1965

9

reached $11 billion[6], or 448 times higher than the $24.5 million market value Berkshire had that year[7].

Even though it seemed impossible for Berkshire to catch up, Buffett's company completely blew past GE over the years. At the end of 2019, GE had a market value of about $97.5 billion, compared to $553.5 billion for Berkshire. Revenues at Berkshire were 167.4% higher than at GE. Reported net income was $81.4 billion at Berkshire in 2019, while GE lost $5.4 billion in the year. However, the net income at Berkshire in 2019 overstated its true annual operating earnings. This was the result of a GAAP accounting rule change that went into effect in 2018 that required companies to recognize unrealized gains and losses on equity securities within net income. Berkshire had unrealized gains on equity securities of $53.7 billion in 2019, after accounting for taxes[8]. The change in value of investments has a meaningful impact on Berkshire over the long term, but the year-to-year change is not important. Excluding the effect of unrealized gains on marketable securities, Berkshire would have reported income of $27.7 billion. While this number is much smaller for Berkshire than the reported net income figure, it is still massive compared to the operations of GE.

1965	General Electric	Berkshire Hathaway
Revenues	$4,941,400,000	$49,300,685
Net Income	$237,300,000	$2,279,206
Market Value	$10,901,048,040	$24,462,227

2019	General Electric	Berkshire Hathaway
Revenues	$95,214,000,000	$254,616,000,000
Net Income	-$5,439,000,000	$81,417,000,000
Market Value	$97,466,406,840	$553,542,450,740

The achievements of Berkshire Hathaway are ridiculous and deserve to be studied intensely. While many books have already been written about

Warren Buffett and his investments, less focus has been placed on financial statement analysis. Since Warren Buffett's success investing in the stock market has been so impressive, the incredible achievements of Berkshire Hathaway itself as a business and as a parent company have been overshadowed in the media. The goal of this book was to focus on the financial statements and regulatory filings of Berkshire Hathaway and its major investments.

III. The Textile Mill
1955-1962

Berkshire Hathaway was formed in 1955 with the merger of Berkshire Fine Spinning Associates and the Hathaway Manufacturing Company[1]. Each of the former companies had histories dating back to the 1800's, and both were major textile manufacturers in New England. The business was capital intensive. Inventories made up 41.6% of assets in 1955, while property, plant, and equipment accounted for 30.2% of the company's assets. Receivables made up another 9.7%[2]. There was little in terms of liabilities to fund these assets, which meant that a large portion of the company's equity was made up of tangible assets[3]. Berkshire earned $300,722 in 1955, which amounted to a return on assets of 0.5%[4]. The company's return on equity was about the same due to the low amount of liabilities.

	1955	% of Assets
Cash	$4,169,413	7.6%
Marketable Securities	$4,332,595	7.8%
Accounts Receivable	$5,343,060	9.7%
Inventories	$22,977,417	41.6%
Total Current Assets	**$36,822,486**	**66.7%**
Other Assets	$1,722,328	3.1%
Property, Plant, and Equipment	$16,655,267	30.2%
Total Assets	**$55,200,081**	**100.0%**
Accounts Payable	$2,334,372	4.2%
Accrued Wages and Salaries	$638,080	1.2%
Accrued State and Local Taxes	$189,053	0.3%
Social Security and Withholding Taxes Payable	$638,820	1.2%
Total Current Liabilities	**$3,800,325**	**6.9%**
Long Term Liabilities	-	-
Total Liabilities	**$3,800,325**	**6.9%**
Common Stock	$11,472,820	20.8%
Capital Surplus	$1,849,611	3.4%
Retained Earnings	$38,077,326	69.0%
Total Stockholders Equity	**$51,399,756**	**93.1%**
Total Liabilities and Stockholders Equity	**$55,200,081**	**100.0%**

At the beginning of 1955, Berkshire was selling for $14.75 per share[5], which valued the company at about $33.8 million[6]. Berkshire had a book value of $51.4 million and net current assets of $33 million[7]. The company

14

was selling for two-thirds of the net worth stated on its books, and close to the value of its working capital net of all liabilities.

	1955
Total Current Assets	$36,822,486
-Total Liabilities	$3,800,325
Net Current Assets	**$33,022,161**
Market Capitalization	$33,844,819
Book Value	$51,399,756
Price to Book Value	65.8%

From 1955 to 1961, profits were tough to come by, as Berkshire posted negative or low single digit profit margins each year, with the exception of 1960. The company cumulatively lost $1.5 million over the period on $441.4 million of sales.[8]

Year	Sales	Net Income	Profit Margin
1955	$65,498,284	$300,722	0.5%
1956	$68,042,770	$922,548	1.4%
1957	$66,098,223	-$3,258,034	-4.9%
1958	$61,956,405	-$4,975,460	-8.0%
1959	$69,511,792	$1,322,099	1.9%
1960	$62,608,679	$4,623,980	7.4%
1961	$47,722,281	-$393,054	-0.8%
Total	**$441,438,434**	**-$1,457,199**	**-0.3%**

Berkshire paid out dividends of $9 million over the seven year period, while not earning any profits in aggregate. Profits would have to increase substantially or else management would be effectively liquidating the

15

company through its dividend payments. The cumulative dividends over that seven year period would have made up almost a quarter of Berkshire's total equity at the end of 1961. The company also returned capital to shareholders through share repurchases. Berkshire spent almost as much on share repurchases over the period as they paid out in dividends. The following table shows just how significant these decisions were in terms of the company's equity. Although the capital structure of Berkshire changed in a big way in the late 1950's, the dividend payments and share repurchases were not sustainable going forward.[9]

Total Equity - 1955	$51,399,756
Dividends 1955-1961	$9,013,531
Share Repurchases 1955-1961	$7,765,935
Total Amount Returned to Shareholders	$16,779,466
Total Equity - 1961	$36,175,695
Returned to Shareholders as % of 1955 Equity	32.6%
Returned to Shareholders as % of 1961 Equity	46.4%

In addition, the company spent $15.1 million on capital expenditures over the period.[10] This money was not spent as an investment to grow the company, but instead was money necessary simply to keep the lights on and remain in business. Sales declined throughout the period as more of shareholders' capital was invested in the business. Management dipped into their excess cash and sold most of the marketable securities they owned in order to pay for these capital expenditures, dividends, and share repurchases.

Year	Sales	YOY Growth*	CAGR**
1955	$65,498,284		
1956	$68,042,770	3.90%	3.90%
1957	$66,098,223	-2.90%	-1.40%
1958	$61,956,405	-6.30%	-2.10%
1959	$69,511,792	12.20%	2.90%
1960	$62,608,679	-9.90%	-2.10%
1961	$47,722,281	-23.80%	-4.40%

*Year-over-year growth rate
**Compound annual growth rate since 1955

Capital expenditures exceeded the amount of depreciation expense the company incurred over the period. Since this was a business that had no growth, this means that depreciation did not quite represent the true replacement cost of assets. Terms like EBITDA would not be appropriate to use when analyzing Berkshire during this period, as more than the entire amount of depreciation was needed to keep the business running. There is no sense in ignoring depreciation when it represents a mandatory expense over the long term.

Year	Capital Expenditures	Depreciation[11]	Difference
1955	$1,201,470	$1,799,447	-$597,977
1956	$1,334,158	$1,895,806	-$561,648
1957	$2,334,356	$1,971,157	$363,199
1958	$1,279,848	$1,941,476	-$661,628
1959	$1,125,253	$1,636,769	-$511,516
1960	$3,818,632	$1,713,004	$2,105,628
1961	$4,020,542	$2,128,699	$1,891,843
Total	$15,114,259	$13,086,358	$2,027,901

> "The directors decided that it would be to the ultimate best interests of the stockholders to permanently close and liquidate the highest cost plants with their obsolete machinery, and to modernize and consolidate the remainder, reducing the total over-all operations to a volume which could be merchandised at a profit after the recession had run its course."
> – 1958 Berkshire Hathaway Annual Report

Berkshire reduced the amount of shares outstanding throughout the period when it repurchased its own stock. Management decided to shut down unprofitable plants and use the proceeds to reinvest in modernized equipment and fund the stock repurchases. The repurchase of stock appeared to be a decent investment for shareholders, at least compared to the alternative uses of capital. These were high cost plants with obsolete machinery, so liquidating them made sense. Management could reinvest the proceeds into more plants and equipment, but those types of operations earned low rates of return in the past. Since this business earned low rates of return on capital, it would make sense to move capital to other businesses that could earn higher rates of return. Returning capital to shareholders was the only satisfactory option remaining due to the fact that management was unwilling to reinvest capital into other types of businesses.

	Shares Repurchased[12]	Shares Outstanding
1955	-	2,294,564
1956	48,450	2,246,114
1957	140,145	2,105,969
1958	-	2,105,969
1959	169,648	1,936,321
1960	310,802	1,625,519
1961	18,139	1,607,380
Total (1955-1961)	**687,184**	

Management could return capital to shareholders either through dividends or by repurchasing its own stock. Over this time period, Berkshire did both. Dividends face a double taxation, as the business pays taxes on the income it earns annually, while the shareholder also pays taxes on the dividends received. During this time period, dividends were taxed at the individual shareholder's income tax rate. When the company repurchases its own stock, continuing shareholders avoid the second form of tax. The company still pays a tax on its income, but wouldn't face any additional taxes when buying back its own stock. Shareholders would just be taxed on capital gains if and when they eventually sold their stock. This means that continuing shareholders could defer taxes through the repurchase option, which is beneficial in many situations.

Although book value and net working capital levels decreased over the period, the per share value of these metrics did better due to the reduction in shares outstanding. While the company's book value decreased by 7.0% from 1959 to 1961, book value per share increased by 12.0%. Net working capital decreased by 23.3%, while net working capital per share only decreased by 7.5%.

	1959	1960	1961	1959-1961[13]
Net Working Capital (NWC)*	$25,858,987	$23,430,319	$19,844,122	
Growth Rate		-9.4%	-15.3%	-23.3%
NWC/Share	$13.35	$14.41	$12.35	
Growth Rate		7.9%	-14.3%	-7.5%
Book Value (BV)	$38,911,549	$37,981,820	$36,175,695	
Growth Rate		-2.4%	-4.8%	-7.0%
BV/Share	$20.10	$23.37	$22.51	
Growth Rate		16.3%	-3.7%	12.0%

*Working capital net of all liabilities

The textiles that Berkshire manufactured were commodity products. Its customers were searching for the lowest cost, and there was no brand or other differentiating aspect that allowed Berkshire to charge premium prices. American textile manufacturers were unable to compete with cheaper labor overseas. According to the 1955 annual report, Japanese workers were paid less than $0.15 per hour, while the minimum wage in the U.S. at the time was $1.00 per hour.[14] The low cost operator wins when producing a commodity product, and Berkshire and its domestic competitors stood no chance against foreign competition in this aspect.

"The rapid increases in imports of cotton fabrics which have occurred recently present a very serious threat to the textile industry and to this Company, and at present, a flood of Japanese fabrics is coming into the United States in ever increasing volume. With wages of less than 15 cents per hour the Japanese can undersell any mill in this country no matter how low its costs may be."
-1955 Berkshire Hathaway Annual Report

Nothing about this business looked attractive, except for the price it was selling for at certain points in time. In 1957, for example, the stock price went down to almost $5 per share.[15] This would have meant a market value of $11.2 million for Berkshire, which was only 22.3% of the company's book value at the end of the most recent year. Berkshire had current assets alone of $41 million against total liabilities of $9.6 million. Even if you ignore the net plant assets the company owned as well as other fixed assets, Berkshire still had current assets of $31.4 million net of all liabilities. This is almost three times higher than where the stock was trading at the 1957 low point. The 1957 value of Berkshire in the market was far below what the business owners could get if they just liquidated the company.

The following table shows one example of the assumptions necessary in order to justify the market value of Berkshire in 1957. In this example, assume the company could only collect 60% of its receivables, the inventory was worth less than a quarter of its book value, the net plant assets could only fetch a third of its carrying value, and all other fixed assets were worthless. If these assumptions held true, Berkshire could still be liquidated for the $11.2 million it was selling for.

	Book Value[16]	Assumptions	% of Book Value
Cash	$2,554,457	$2,554,457	100.0%
Accounts Receivable	$7,136,305	$4,281,783	60.0%
Marketable Securities	$482,288	$482,288	100.0%
Inventories	$30,842,230	$7,847,512	23.0%
Other Fixed Assets	$1,812,116	-	0.0%
Net Plant Assets	$17,131,036	$5,653,242	33.0%
Total Liabilities	-$9,588,712	-$9,588,712	100.0%
Net Assets	**$50,369,720**	**$11,230,570**	**22.3%**

While Berkshire was less than impressive as a company, these assumptions really would have been pessimistic. The company's fixed assets were comprised of land, buildings, machinery, equipment, investments in unconsolidated subsidiaries, and other assets. It is unlikely that all of these assets would be liquidated for such little value. Even though this was a bad business, the company was selling for far too low of a price during this period. Eventually the market value recovered to $27.4 million during 1959[17], gaining 143.8% from the low of 1957. An investment in Berkshire at the low valuation of 1957 would have enjoyed a compound annual growth rate of 56.1% over a two year period. This market price was close to the value of the company's current assets net of all liabilities in 1959. Although much more reasonable, it was still a modest valuation of the business.

IV. The Investment
1962 - 1965

Warren Buffett bought his first shares of Berkshire Hathaway for $7.51 per share near the end of 1962.[1] By the end of 2019, the stock price of Berkshire was $339,590 per share. At the time, he was the general partner of Buffett Partnership, Limited (BPL). This was basically a hedge fund before the term was commonly used. Buffett raised money from investors to buy stocks he viewed as undervalued. People who decided to invest had to keep their money in the partnership for a year. At the end of each year, they had the option to withdraw their money or remain invested for another 12 months. Berkshire Hathaway was one of the many cheap stocks that Buffett found for the partnership.

At the end of 1962, Berkshire had $16.5 million in current assets net of all liabilities, and a book value of $32.5 million.[2] The company had a market value of $12.1 million based on the $7.51 per share initial purchase price that Buffett paid. This valuation meant that Berkshire was selling for about 73.3% of net current assets and 37.2% of book value. Additionally, Berkshire had unused tax loss carryforwards worth $4.5 million at the end of 1962 due to the losses reported in previous years.[3] Since Berkshire was only valued at $12.1 million, this potential tax shield could be valuable. The only problem was that Berkshire first needed to become profitable in order to enjoy the benefits of the tax loss carryforward. The tax benefit would expire within five years, so at the time it would have been unclear how much of this tax shield could be used.

While the stock was clearly statistically cheap, the income statement provided a good argument for the cheap valuation. The company was struggling to make a profit, losing $2.2 million in 1962. Sales were $53.3 million, down 23.4% from 1959.[4] Additionally, net current assets and book value decreased 47.6% and 35.5%, respectively, from 1956 until Buffett's investment in 1962. This decrease was mainly due to two reasons. First, Berkshire lost $4.8 million over the period. Second, the company liquidated certain assets and used the excess cash to repurchase stock and pay dividends. Shares outstanding decreased 28.4%, from 2,246,114 in 1956 to 1,607,380 in 1962 due to these repurchases.[5]

24

Management followed through with their 1958 promise to close and liquidate unprofitable plants. Berkshire reiterated that its plan was to use those funds to continue repurchasing its own stock. If Berkshire's stock was selling for too low of a valuation, then buying back its own shares below fair value would be a good investment.

> "Berkshire Hathaway continues to be in a strong financial position, and it is expected that the Company will have current assets in excess of its requirements during the coming year because of the decrease in the number of plants operated and the anticipated reduction in our inventories. It would seem prudent, under the circumstances, to use the excess assets to reduce the number of shares of stock outstanding."
> – 1962 Berkshire Hathaway Annual Report

> "Charlie and I favor repurchases when two conditions are met: first, a company has ample funds to take care of the operational and liquidity needs of its business; second, its stock is selling at a material discount to the company's intrinsic business value, conservatively calculated."
> – Warren Buffett's 2011 Letter to Berkshire Hathaway Shareholders[6]

Management at Berkshire believed that the first condition was met, as they had current assets in excess of what was required. Buffett apparently believed the second condition was met, as he bought Berkshire stock because he viewed it as undervalued. After Berkshire repurchased its shares, continuing shareholders would own a larger percentage of this undervalued company without having to put up more of their own money. Also, this situation created a potential catalyst for an increasing stock price. Since Berkshire was a relatively small company with a low amount of volume being traded on its stock, an organization buying large blocks of stock may need to increase its asking price in order to fulfill the entire purchase.

· Eventually, BPL owned a large chunk of Berkshire. Since management was looking to buy back more stock, Seabury Stanton, the President and Chairman, eventually discussed a transaction with Buffett. Berkshire agreed to buy BPL's stock at a price of $11.50 per share. When the official offer arrived in the mail shortly thereafter, Berkshire offered to buy back their stock for only $11.375 per share. Instead of accepting the new offer, BPL continued to buy enough stock to take control of the company.[7] By 1965, BPL owned over half of the company, and Buffett joined the board of Berkshire.[8]

BPL began buying stock in Berkshire at $7.51 per share. Seabury Stanton's original offer of $11.50 would have meant a gain of 53.1% for BPL from that initial price. The final offer still would have meant a gain of 51.5%. This gain would have been achieved in about a year and a half from the original purchase. BPL probably paid more than $7.51 per share as it built up its position in Berkshire, but this additional investment was invested for less time before Seabury Stanton's offer.

Buffett could have taken the proceeds and continued to invest in undervalued stocks. Instead, he was about to learn his lesson in acquiring poor businesses that appeared undervalued statistically. By early 1966, BPL owned 552,528 shares or 54.3% of the company.[9] This stake in Berkshire was acquired at an average cost of $14.86 per share, reflecting higher prices paid by BPL in 1965.[10] Buffett was now stuck with this bad business, and would later comment that it was his worst investment decision.

"As of January 21, 1966 Buffett Partnership, Ltd., a limited partnership under Nebraska law, owned approximately 54.3% of Registrant's outstanding shares. Mr. Warren E. Buffett, a director of the Registrant, is the sole general partner of the partnership."
- 1965 Berkshire Hathaway Annual Report

V. The Transition
1965 – 1967

Warren Buffett took over Berkshire Hathaway in 1965, acquiring control of the stock and joining the board of directors. In this role, he began allocating capital in a legendary way. The effects were immediately felt at Berkshire.

In 1964, all of the company's capital was invested in textile operations. As I previously stated, this type of business historically produced low returns on investment. Buffett moved some capital to stocks, and then later to insurance and banking operations. He was able to come up with excess capital to reinvest due to cash generated from the sale of equipment, a reduction in inventory, and from profits produced in 1965 and 1966. The profits generated in those two years were mostly due to efficient cost cutting achieved once Buffett took over as Chairman.

> "The Corporation made a substantial reduction in its overhead costs during the fiscal year just ended."
> – 1965 Berkshire Hathaway Annual Report

	1964	1965
Sales	$49,982,830	$49,300,685
Growth		-1.4%
Cost of Sales	$47,382,337	$42,478,984
Growth		-10.3%

In Buffett's first year controlling Berkshire, the cost of sales decreased by 10.3% while sales only decreased 1.4%.[1] The annual report pointed out that a substantial reduction in overhead costs was achieved during the year.[2] The reduction in costs was very meaningful for Berkshire in terms of overall dollars. The cost of sales declined by $4.9 million in 1965, while total profits were only $175,586 in 1964.[3] This cost savings was almost 28 times higher than Berkshire's total profits from the year before, and was over 12 times more than net income before special items. In 1964, special items included idle plant expense of $226,025.[4]

The cost control Berkshire achieved in 1965 helped the company generate cash to deploy elsewhere, and this was an important first step in building Berkshire into one of the great companies of the world. The business would have reported little to no profits under the old cost structure. However, more capital was being destroyed than what was reported on the income statement in 1964. Berkshire charged $3 million against retained earnings for estimated losses on properties to be sold in 1964.[5] This $3 million charge did not hit the income statement, but instead reduced shareholder's equity. Berkshire had write-downs totaling $6.2 million from 1962 to 1965 for losses on properties to be sold.[6] Net income would have amounted to a loss of $2.8 million in 1964 after taking into account special items as well as write-downs.

In 1965 and 1966, the textile operations produced net income of $2.3 million and $2.8 million, respectively.[7] Unlike the situation from 1962 to 1964, the reported net income understated the cash profits earned by the company in 1965 and 1966. Due to tax loss carryforwards from unprofitable years in the past, the profits earned by Berkshire in 1965 and 1966 were not taxed. Berkshire still reported an expense on the income statement for taxes to avoid misleading investors about the true profitability of the business going forward.[8] The income statement listed $2 million and $2.2 million of expenses for income taxes in 1965 and 1966, respectively. Ignoring this tax expense, since it didn't actually have to be paid, would mean Berkshire actually earned cash profits of $4.3 million in 1965 and $5 million in 1966.

	1965	1966
Net Income	$2,279,206	$2,762,514
+ Provision for Taxes	$2,040,000	$2,242,000
+ Depreciation	$862,424	$963,000
- Capital Expenditures	-$811,812	-$970,000
Free Cash Flow	**$4,369,818**	**$4,997,514**

In both 1965 and 1966, capital expenditures were close to the depreciation charge that Berkshire had on its income statement. This means that free cash flow was pretty close to the reported net income value over the period, excluding the provision for taxes. The $4.4 million of free cash flow in 1965 made up a large portion of the capital Berkshire was able to generate that year. The remainder of capital came from a decrease in inventory and property, plant, and equipment. An increase in accounts payable on the liability side provided some benefit as well. Property, plant, and equipment on the balance sheet decreased by $953,796 year-over-year.[9] A portion of the reduction in property, plant, and equipment was due to a write-down of $300,000 though.[10] This write-down just reflected a reduction in carrying value instead of actual capital being generated from the textile business. Berkshire also reported less cash on the balance sheet at year end. In 1966, free cash flow increased to $5 million, but this was partially offset by an increase in inventory for the year. Ignoring the increase in marketable securities and the decrease in debt, the following table shows the changes in capital invested within the textile operations. Marketable securities were removed from current assets in the table because the line item constitutes an investment outside of the textile industry. The change in debt was ignored because it was a change in the capital structure instead of an investment decision within the textile business.

	1964	1965	1966
Net Textile Current Assets	$20,250,361	$18,671,799	$21,113,650
- Net Textile Current Liabilities	$3,248,293	$3,702,273	$3,401,258
Net Textile Working Capital	**$17,002,068**	**$14,969,526**	**$17,712,392**
+ Fixed Assets	$7,636,685	$6,650,588	$6,336,733
Capital Invested in Textiles	**$24,638,753**	**$21,620,114**	**$24,049,125**
Change in Capital Invested in Textiles		**-$3,018,639**	**$2,429,011**

	1965	1966
Free Cash Flow	$4,369,818	$4,997,514
+ Capital Generated from Textiles	$3,018,639	-$2,429,011
- Write-down of PPE	-$300,000	
Total Capital Generated	**$7,088,457**	**$2,568,503**

Free cash flow in 1965 and 1966 combined to a value of $9.4 million. This level of free cash flow amounted to 77.6% of the $12.1 million valuation Berkshire had when Buffett first invested in 1962. This free cash flow represented 55.4% of the average cost Buffett paid for Berkshire, which valued the company at $16.9 million. Total capital generated from textiles in 1965 alone amounted to $7.1 million, or 41.9% of the average cost Buffett paid for Berkshire.

31

Most business managers would have taken this capital generated from the textile business and reinvested it right back into their normal operations. Maybe they would pay out a small dividend on the side. This is mostly what Berkshire had done throughout its history. This changed once Buffett gained control of Berkshire. The company became debt free after paying off its $2.5 million debenture in 1965.[11] Also, Berkshire reported $2.9 million of marketable securities on the balance sheet in 1965 after having none the previous year.[12] The company added funds to the marketable securities portfolio in 1966, as Berkshire reported $5.4 million of marketable securities at cost on the balance sheet.[13] Berkshire also repurchased some of its own stock in 1965[14], reducing the shares outstanding from 1,137,778[15] to 1,017,547[16].

Uses of Capital	1965	1966
Purchase of Marketable Securities	$2,900,000	$2,545,795
Reduction of Debt	$2,500,000	-
Share Repurchases	$1,637,844	-
Total	**$7,037,844**	**$2,545,795**

The annual report in 1966 provides a breakdown of how the marketable securities were invested. Bonds accounted for 88.1% of the portfolio, with the remainder in common stocks.[17] Berkshire acquired its first insurance company, National Indemnity, in 1967. Buffett could have been searching for an acquisition in the few years leading up to purchasing National Indemnity. This could potentially explain the heavy allocation to bonds during this period. The portfolio was entirely made up of common stocks in 1967 after completing the acquisition.[18]

"Four years ago your management committed itself to the development of more substantial and more consistent earning power than appeared possible if capital continued to be invested exclusively in the textile industry. The funds for this program were temporarily utilized in marketable securities, pending the acquisition of operating businesses meeting our investment and management criteria."
-Warren Buffett's 1969 Letter to Berkshire Hathaway Shareholders

It is difficult to overstate how important it was that Berkshire generated this capital in 1965 and 1966. Berkshire's textile business was shut down in 1985, but was struggling for many years before this. Other business owners might have shut down the textile operation much sooner. 250 textile mills closed from 1980 to 1985.[19] If Berkshire never allocated capital away from textiles, then the enterprise wouldn't exist today. Berkshire and its subsidiaries had 391,500 employees[20] at the end of 2019, and the company spent $16 billion on capital expenditures[21] that year alone. These capital expenditures were spent repairing railroads, building wind power plants, buying equipment, and much more. This provides jobs for employees outside of Berkshire as well. The U.S. government received $243 billion from corporate income taxes in 2019, and Berkshire paid 1.5% of this total.[22] Due to its prudent management and financial conservatism, the company has also provided the economy with excess capital in times of need. In difficult time periods, such as the financial crisis of 2008 and 2009, Berkshire provided liquidity to companies like GE and Goldman Sachs. When supply tightens in the insurance industry, Berkshire is there to write premiums to those who need it.

Berkshire historically sold for a discount to book value, but at this point in time some of its new assets were worth more than their carrying value. Cash and marketable securities made up 13% of assets in 1965.[23] This increased to over 18.5% of assets in 1966.[24] The stocks and bonds owned by Berkshire were reported on the balance sheet at cost, but had market values that at times were much higher. After being only slightly greater in 1966, the market value of the portfolio in 1967 was $6.8 million compared to a cost of

33

only $3.9 million.[25] This was due to large unrealized gains in the value of the company's stocks. Berkshire reported a cumulative operating profit of $9.6 million from 1965 to 1967[26], excluding dividends, interest, and realized gains from marketable securities, so this gain of $3 million in the portfolio was meaningful. Additionally, this operating profit excludes interest expense, income taxes, and non-recurring expenses such as idle plant expense. Reported assets totaled $38 million in 1967, but would have been 7.9% higher if marketable securities were reported at fair value.[27]

In 1964, Berkshire sold for between 45.1% and 71.7% of book value.[28] In 1965, it sold for between 69.4% and 110.5% of book value.[29] Even though the company was going through a major transition, Berkshire still sold for between 56.9% and 70.7% of book value in 1967.[30] If the balance sheet included marketable securities at fair value, the valuation[31] of Berkshire would have been 66.1% of book value at the low end of 1968.[32] The cash and marketable securities being discussed were held at the parent company level, and not within the insurance company. Berkshire reported its insurance operation as an unconsolidated subsidiary because it was such a different type of business than textiles. Due to this, the following table[33] does not include its portfolio within the insurance companies. The portfolio of the parent company was mostly liquidated in 1969 in order to acquire the Illinois National Bank & Trust Company of Rockford, Illinois.

Marketable Securities	Cost	Market Value	% Gain
1964	-	-	-
1965	$2,900,000	*	*
1966	$5,445,795	$5,458,238	0.2%
1967	$3,856,517	$6,845,000	77.5%
1968	$5,421,384	$11,824,000	118.1%
1969	$294,165	$297,120	1.0%

*Not disclosed in Annual Report

It is interesting to look back at the valuation of Berkshire in 1967. The company was selling for between $16.8 million and $20.9 million throughout the year.[34] In March of that year, Berkshire paid $8.6 million to buy National Indemnity.[35] Investors at the time might have disagreed about the valuation of National Indemnity, but Buffett was already a legendary investor by then with a great track record. Assume the $8.6 million Buffett paid was a fair value for the company. Berkshire also owned stocks with a fair value of $5.5 million. Combining these two pieces would give you $14.1 million, or 83.9% of Berkshire's valuation at the low end of 1967. This implies that Berkshire's textile operations were almost worthless. The textile operations usually sold at a large discount, but the market never before implied that the business was completely worthless. After taking into account National Indemnity and the portfolio of stocks, this left $2.7 million of valuation to account for. Berkshire had receivables of $8.1 million, inventory of $12.2 million, and net plant assets of $6.3 million. If you take these assets against the total liabilities of $3.4 million, you come to a net value of $23.2 million for textile assets when the market was implying around $2.7 million.[36] Additionally, the reduction in overhead and the gains achieved on the marketable securities portfolio over the previous few years were very impressive. The market could have assumed Buffett's ability to do this was maxed out, as Berkshire's valuation was being given no premium for this in the market. Another explanation would be that few people realized the extent of the changes taking place within Berkshire at the time.

A major part of the transition at Berkshire over this period took place within the company's marketable securities portfolio. At the end of 1966, 87.9% of Berkshire's portfolio of marketable securities was invested in bonds and the remainder in stocks. Of the stocks, 56.9% was invested in Investors Diversified Services (IDS), 26.7% in Walt Disney Productions, 8.3% in John Blair & Company, and 8.2% Massachusetts Indemnity & Life Insurance Company.[37] The 1967 annual report disclosed the addition of American Express, Florida Gas Company, Sperry and Hutchinson, and Rank Organization. Wrigley and the Crompton Company were added in 1968,

35

bringing the number of stocks up to 10. Bonds were reduced to 11.3% of the portfolio by 1968, and the top three stocks made up 68.5% of the portfolio based on market value. American Express made up 29.2%, while 20.5% was invested in Sperry and Hutchinson, followed by 18.8% in IDS.[38]

1966	Shares	% of Portfolio	Cost	Market Value
John Blair & Company	3,300	1.0%	$48,825	$54,450
Walt Disney Productions	3,900	3.2%	$168,651	$175,500
Investors Diversified Services A	13,371	6.9%	$374,528	$374,388
Massachusetts Indemnity & Life Insurance Company	2,200	1.0%	$55,462	$53,900
Bonds	-	87.9%	$4,798,329	$4,800,000
Total			**$5,445,795**	**$5,458,238**

1968	% of Portfolio	Cost	Market Value	% Gain
American Express	29.2%	$1,065,000	3,454,000	224.3%
John Blair & Company	5.8%	$227,880	$683,000	199.7%
Walt Disney Productions	10.5%	$290,669	$1,247,000	329.0%
Florida Gas Company	0.1%	$6,504	$10,000	53.8%
Investors Diversified Services A	18.5%	$1,162,456	$2,191,000	88.5%
Investors Diversified Services B	0.2%	$14,962	$29,000	93.8%
Massachusetts Indemnity & Life Insurance Company	0.8%	$55,462	$99,000	78.5%
Rank Organization	1.2%	$37,977	$137,000	260.7%
Sperry & Hutchinson	20.5%	$1,036,209	$2,429,000	134.4%
Crompton Company	0.2%	$23,203	$26,000	12.1%
Wm. Wrigley, Jr.	1.6%	$165,902	$184,000	10.9%
Bonds	11.3%	$1,335,160	$1,335,000	0.0%
Total		$5,421,384	$11,824,000	118.1%

During this period, Berkshire's marketable securities portfolio performed extremely well as all of the stocks gained in value. The worst stock, which was Wrigley on a cumulative basis, went up 10.9%. Walt Disney went up 329%. Rank Organization went up 260.7%, while American Express went up 224.3%. This portfolio of stocks gained a total of $6.4 million in value during 1967 and 1968, while textile operations only produced pretax operating profits[39] of $2.2 million over the same period.[40] Berkshire's portfolio of stocks made a meaningful impact on the bottom line, and helped to fund the initial expansion of Berkshire into other businesses.

VI. The Acquisitions
1967 - 1969

National Indemnity

"In March 1967, the Company purchased for $8,577,000 over 99% of the outstanding stock of National Indemnity Company and 100% of the outstanding stock of National Fire & Marine Insurance Company, both headquartered in Omaha, Nebraska."
– 1967 Berkshire Hathaway Annual Report

National Indemnity was founded by Jack Ringwalt in 1940.[1] The business and its affiliate company, National Fire & Marine, shared an office in Omaha. The companies were involved in property and casualty insurance, with the majority of their premiums generated in the automotive field at the time of Berkshire's acquisition.[2] The National Indemnity acquisition marked the first time Berkshire allocated capital away from textiles and into a fully owned business operating in a different industry. While this would provide some diversity in earnings for Berkshire, there were many other attractive aspects of National Indemnity.

Insurance is a business in which companies collect premiums first and pay claims later. This timing difference allows insurers to earn money investing funds that will have to be paid out to policyholders eventually. These funds are referred to as "float". National Indemnity didn't have any debt in terms of loans from a bank. Banks charge interest, demand full repayment at a specified date, and have recourse if the loan is not paid back. National Indemnity was still able to enjoy the use of leverage through float and other liabilities.

"The float figures are derived from the total of loss reserves, loss adjustment expense reserves and unearned premium reserves minus agents' balances, prepaid acquisition costs and deferred charges applicable to assumed reinsurance."
– Warren Buffett's 1990 Letter to Berkshire Hathaway Shareholders

40

In 1955, a decade before Berkshire's investment, National Indemnity had $1.5 million of equity. The company had $4.9 million of assets though, as $3.4 million of capital was funded by liabilities. About $2 million, or 58.1% of the total liabilities, were from float. Stocks made up $1.4 million on the asset side, which was close to the value of the firm's equity or shareholders' funds. The policyholders' funds were mostly made up of bonds and cash. National Indemnity earned $204,607 of net income on about $2 million of premiums. This amounted to a return on equity of 13.3%, which is far higher than the 0.6% Berkshire Hathaway earned in 1955.[3] Berkshire's textile business earned slightly more profits that year, with net income of $300,722.[4] However, Berkshire needed $51.4 million of equity[5] to earn that level of income, compared to just $1.5 million of equity for National Indemnity.[6] National Indemnity was far more efficient with its capital.

National Indemnity[7]	1955	1960	1965
Loss Reserves	$1,137,226	$3,336,599	$7,267,320
Loss Adjustment Expense Reserves	$209,957	$1,040,389	$2,114,627
Unearned Premiums	$875,807	$3,302,283	$5,322,544
Agents' Balances (Asset)	-$268,606	-$842,389	-$293,219
Reinsurance Recoverable (Asset)	-	-$139,206	-$1,017,694
Total Float	**$1,954,384**	**$6,697,676**	**$13,393,578**
Float CAGR		27.9%	21.2%

National Indemnity[8]	1955	1960	1965
Underwriting Gain	$98,934	$150,205	$40,793
Investment Gain	$229,559	$392,371	$1,157,739
Other Gain (Loss)	-$982	-$11,458	-$4,259
Pretax Income	$327,511	$531,118	$1,194,273
Income Taxes	$122,904	$149,277	$311,073
Net Income	$204,607	$381,841	$883,200
Net Income CAGR		13.3%	15.7%

Over the next 10 years, National Indemnity prospered. Growth in premiums registered at 21.3% compounded annually, while net income compounded at a rate of 15.7%. The average return on equity was 11.2%. Float grew 21.2% compounded annually to a value of $13.4 million. Most importantly, the float was obtained with disciplined underwriting standards, as it was cost-free in 6 of the 10 years. The combined ratio ranged from a low of 91.2% in 1959 to 102.3% in 1962. A combined ratio of 100% basically means that the firm broke even from underwriting before taking into account any investment income. In 1965, for example, the combined ratio was 99.9%, with 67.4% from losses on policies, and the other 32.5% of expenses coming from overhead.[9] The majority of this overhead came from commissions and brokerage expenses paid in order to acquire business. When someone goes to a bank to borrow money, they have to pay interest on that loan. National Indemnity was able to borrow $13.4 million from policyholders in 1965 and earned a 0.1% fee for borrowing this money. Even when the cost of float reached a high of 102.3% in 1962, this still meant that National Indemnity was only paying 2.3% interest to borrow money from policyholders. With the 10 year treasury bond yielding 3.9% in 1962, this was a low-cost source of funding.[10] Basically, the U.S. Government was borrowing at a rate of almost 4% while National Indemnity was borrowing at 2% or less. The ability of some firms to get paid to borrow money has attracted the attention of many over the years, leading to tough competition in the insurance industry.

42

	1955	1960	1965
Loss Ratio	59.6%	66.6%	67.4%
Underwriting Ratio	35.2%	31.5%	32.5%
Combined Ratio	94.8%	98.1%	99.9%
Total Float	$1,954,384	$6,697,676	$13,393,578

	1955	1960	1965
Amount "Borrowed"	$1,954,384	$6,697,676	$13,393,578
Interest Rate	-5.2%	-1.9%	-0.1%

Berkshire paid $8.6 million in order to acquire National Indemnity in early 1967. National Indemnity and National Fire & Marine had combined equity totaling $6.7 million.[11] National Indemnity alone earned $1.4 million[12] the year before, but that was an outlier as the average net income over the previous 12 years was $437,000. Based on the net income earned in 1966, the price paid for National Indemnity looks like a bargain, yielding 16.6%. If you used the average net income over the previous dozen years, the yield is a much more reasonable 5.1%. Additionally, National Fire & Marine was earning profits as well. Although it is unclear its earning level prior to the acquisition, the company earned $164,000 before realized gains on investments in 1967.[13] If you add this figure to the 12 year average National Indemnity profits, it would give Berkshire an immediate yield of 7% based on its purchase price. It would be reasonable to assume that the investment results of National Indemnity would improve once Buffett took control of the company. He had already achieved more than a decade of outstanding results running BPL. Even if Buffett could only improve the investment income earned on National Indemnity's float by 1%, this would result in $175,024 of additional income for the company in 1967. $175,024 would be 2% of Berkshire's purchase price for National Indemnity. Additionally, any growth in float could lead to additional investment income. This shows that even small improvements to the investment portfolio could be meaningful based on Berkshire's purchase price.

National Indemnity would also benefit over the long term by being owned within a diversified holding company. Berkshire had additional capital outside of the insurance industry. In 1966, National Indemnity earned premiums of $16 million. The total equity under U.S. GAAP accounting was $5.6 million.[14] This means that National Indemnity wrote premiums of almost three times higher than its equity. This is referred to as operating leverage. While leverage magnifies gains in good times, it also magnifies losses. Excluding the effect of investment income, a combined ratio of 117 during a particularly bad year would wipe out over half of the company's equity when it is leveraged by a factor of three. The company's consistent underwriting discipline would suggest that a combined ratio of 117 was unlikely, but it still could have been possible someday down the road. While the company had no financial leverage in terms of debt, it was pretty leveraged in terms of its operations. If National Indemnity or the insurance industry experienced tough times, Berkshire could potentially use its additional capital to help the business fund the commitments it made to policyholders.

"Before I discuss our 2017 insurance results, let me remind you of how and why we entered the field. We began by purchasing National Indemnity and a smaller sister company for $8.6 million in early 1967. With our purchase we received $6.7 million of tangible net worth that, by the nature of the insurance business, we were able to deploy in marketable securities. It was easy to rearrange the portfolio into securities we would otherwise have owned at Berkshire itself. In effect, we were "trading dollars" for the net worth portion of the cost.

The $1.9 million premium over net worth that Berkshire paid brought us an insurance business that usually delivered an underwriting profit. Even more important, the insurance operation carried with it $19.4 million of "float" – money that belonged to others but was held by our two insurers."
- Warren Buffett's 2017 Letter to Berkshire Hathaway Shareholders

In his 2017 letter to Berkshire shareholders, Buffett discussed the acquisition of National Indemnity with a unique point of view. National Indemnity's tangible net worth, or $6.7 million, could be ignored in terms of the purchase price. Whether this $6.7 million was kept within Berkshire or used to buy National Indemnity was irrelevant because Buffett would have invested this money in the same stocks either way. Ignoring the tangible net worth leaves $1.9 million of goodwill that Berkshire paid for the company. This $1.9 million of goodwill would allow Berkshire to reap the benefits of any underwriting gain earned by National Indemnity, as well as the investment income earned on the float. If you assume Buffett could earn income of 5% on the float, then that would amount to $780,982 annually or 41.1% of the $1.9 million of goodwill.[15] On the other hand, many insurance companies lose money from underwriting. If National Indemnity's underwriting results declined, then any underwriting loss would take away from the investment income earned on the float. In the end, the success of the National Indemnity acquisition depended on just two variables. The first variable was how much float would be generated, and the second was what the cost of that float would be over time. The price paid for National Indemnity looks extremely attractive based on this perspective. On average, National Indemnity produced a small underwriting profit from 1955 to 1966. This means that the float was better than cost-free. If this type of underwriting could continue, then Berkshire only needed to earn 1.8% on its float in order to produce a return of 15% per year based on the $1.9 million of goodwill paid for National Indemnity. As long as National Indemnity didn't start producing large underwriting losses, this acquisition looks like a major winner.

It is important to note that the calculation for float can vary from company to company and from analyst to analyst. The exact value for the float is unimportant. The calculation does not need to be carried out to the last decimal place. However, it is crucial to understand roughly what type of leverage from policyholders an insurance company operates with. In Buffett's 2017 letter to Berkshire shareholders, he wrote that National

Indemnity had $19.4 million in float around the time of the acquisition. I assume this is referring to the float at the end of 1967. The 1990 letter to Berkshire shareholders lists $17.3 million as the average float for 1967. The float disclosed by Berkshire does not match the value of float used in this book, but the values are close enough though. The reason for the difference in float calculation is probably due to the treatment of 'Other Assets' and 'Other Liabilities'. It is difficult for an outsider to tell how much of these 'Other' line items are related to policyholders. According to the calculation used in this book, National Indemnity had about $15.6 million of float at the end of 1966, and this is likely to be the figure that investors would have seen in early 1967 when Berkshire made the acquisition.

By acquiring National Indemnity, Berkshire was able to shift capital from textiles to a business that earned much higher returns on equity. Buffett would get his hands on low-cost float, which he could invest in stocks, bonds, or eventually whole businesses. This acquisition marked a big change at Berkshire. Although it was probably unprecedented for a textile manufacturer to acquire an insurance company, it was the best move in terms of being a steward of shareholders' capital.

To fund the National Indemnity acquisition, Berkshire moved more capital away from textiles, sold a portion of its portfolio of marketable securities, and issued long term debt. After this move, the capital Berkshire had invested in textiles was the lowest since Buffett took control of the company. Receivables decreased by $0.9 million in 1967, while accounts payable increased by $1.9 million. Inventory dropped by $1.1 million, and property, plant, and equipment fell by $0.7 million.[16] In total, this amounts to $4.6 million of capital that Berkshire was able to take out of textiles that year. The marketable securities portfolio on the balance sheet was reduced by $1.6 million as investments were sold in order to fund the acquisition. The company reported $2.6 million of debt on the balance sheet in 1967 as well. This debt was a long term source of funding, as it wasn't due until 20 years later in 1987.[17] Berkshire paid 7.5% interest on the debt, which makes National Indemnity's cost of float look even more attractive. The debt

46

offering authorized $9 million of borrowings, so Berkshire had the option to borrow further if the need for more liquidity happened to arise.[18]

	1966	1967	Change
Receivables	$8,114,240	$7,167,884	-$946,356
Inventory	$12,239,261	$11,162,106	-$1,077,155
Net Plant Assets	$6,306,526	$5,610,451	-$696,075
Accounts Payable	$2,957,565	$4,827,079	$1,869,514
Capital Generated from Textiles			**$4,589,100**

Funding for National Indemnity	1967
Capital Generated from Textiles	$4,589,100
Increase in Debt	$2,629,120
Sale of Marketable Securities	$1,589,278
Total	**$8,803,272**

In the mid 1960's, State Farm and Allstate were the largest property and casualty insurance companies in the U.S in terms of premiums. State Farm had premiums of $803.2 million in the property and casualty field in 1964, while Allstate had premiums of $678.3 million that same year.[19] State Farm was 63.2 times larger than National Indemnity, as the company had only $12.7 million of net premiums written in 1964.[20] Berkshire Hathaway was the second largest insurer in the U.S. in 2019 based on premiums written, trailing only State Farm.[21] The National Indemnity acquisition marked a turning point not only within the insurance industry, but within all of American business.

47

Sun Newspaper and Blacker Printing Company

> "Immediately after year end, we purchased all of the stock of Sun Newspapers, Inc. and Blacker Printing Company, Inc., which represents an initial entry into the publishing business."
> – 1968 Berkshire Hathaway Annual Report

The Sun Newspaper published papers in Omaha on weekdays, and had a customer base of about 50,000 at the time.[22] The Blacker Printing Company was a related printing business for the paper. Although there was little information disclosed about this acquisition, it was clear that it was very minor as a percentage of assets or in terms of earnings.

In Berkshire Hathaway's 1969 annual report, the company disclosed a breakdown of its unconsolidated subsidiaries. From this report, we can tell that Berkshire acquired Sun Newspaper for a cost of $626,000 and the Blacker Printing Company for $600,000. Also, the Gateway Underwriters Agency, which was a General Agent for National Indemnity in the state of Missouri, had a cost of $35,000.[23] Berkshire combined all three of these subsidiaries on the balance sheet into 'Other Unconsolidated Subsidiaries'. In 1969, the other unconsolidated subsidiaries line item amounted to 2.2% of total assets.[24] By 1972, the line item made up only 1.5%.[25]

> "The combined investment in Sun, Blacker Printing and Gateway Underwriters is a little over $1 per share of Berkshire Hathaway, and earns something less than 10 cents per share. We have no particular plans to expand in the communication field."
> -Warren Buffett's 1969 BPL Letter to Partners

When he was winding down his partnerships in the late 60's, Buffett disclosed that Sun Newspaper, Blacker Printing, and Gateway Underwriters made up over $1 per share of Berkshire, and that they earned less than $0.10

per share combined.[26] Berkshire had a book value of $45 per share at the time, giving further evidence that these businesses were not material to Berkshire.[27]

The Sun Newspaper was unimpressive financially, and the business was sold in 1980. The paper stopped publishing in 1983.[28] At the time, the newspaper business could be characterized as a winner-takes-all industry. The Sun was by no means the winner in Omaha. The Omaha World Herald was the leader in the area, and enjoyed far better economics. However, this investment may have helped provide insights into the newspaper industry that would prove useful later on at Berkshire.

Illinois National Bank

> "On April 3, 1969, Berkshire Hathaway Inc. acquired 81,989 shares, out of a total of 100,000 shares outstanding, of the common stock of the Illinois National Bank and Trust Co. of Rockford, Illinois, at a cash price of $190.00 per share. They also have made a tender offer to acquire the remaining outstanding shares at the same cash price."
> – 1968 Berkshire Hathaway Annual Report

The Illinois National Bank and Trust Company was a commercial bank that operated in Rockford, Illinois. It was the largest bank in the city of Rockford at the time.[29] The state of Illinois had unusually strict banking laws back then, as each bank was only allowed to operate a single office. In other states, banks typically had many branches that customers could stop into and conduct business. These restrictions were in place until the early 1990's.

> "This bank had been built by Eugene Abegg, without addition of outside capital, from $250,000 of net worth and $400,000 of deposits in 1931 to $17 million of net worth and $100 million of deposits in 1969. Mr. Abegg has continued as Chairman and produced record operating earnings (before security losses) of approximately $2 million in 1969."
> -Warren Buffett's 1969 Letter to Berkshire Hathaway Shareholders

Similar to National Indemnity, Illinois National was able to employ leverage without going into debt in terms of a traditional loan. In this case, the bank accepted deposits from customers, creating a liability on the balance sheet. The bank invested other people's money, making loans or investing in bonds. Illinois National was conservative, and its level of liquidity was unique. Its demand deposits, which customers could withdraw at short notice, were covered on the asset side by cash and safe, short-term government bonds. Total deposits were $99.1 million in 1968, with demand deposits representing $57.7 million of the total. Illinois National had cash and U.S. Government bonds of $68 million, which is far more liquidity than the bank would reasonably expect to need in the short term.[30] The bank had more than enough cash and low-risk bonds to cover any amount of withdrawals of demand deposits. Most banks would have been far more aggressive with these deposits by having a higher percentage of loans. However, this liquidity of Illinois National would protect it in the case of an economic downturn.

In 1960, almost a decade before the acquisition, the bank had deposits of $78.5 million. These deposits made up 96.7% of the company's total liabilities. The bank took in these deposits from customers, along with the $7.7 million of equity in the business, to fund their assets. These assets consisted of $39.1 million of loans, $26.3 million of government bonds, and $9.5 million of municipal or other bonds. The bank also had $13.1 million in cash. This means that the bank had 16.7% of its total deposits backed by cash, and another 45.6% was backed by low-risk bonds. The rest of the deposits were used to make loans, which earned higher interest income than bonds.[31] The bank remained similarly financed throughout the mid 1960's.[32]

	1960	1964	1968
Cash	$13,133,000	$19,495,000	$23,244,160
Government Bonds	$26,280,000	$23,705,000	$26,922,563
Municipal and Other Bonds	$9,481,000	$13,772,000	$17,803,334
Loans	$39,147,000	$53,475,000	$46,995,450
Other Assets	$839,000	$971,000	$2,342,767
Total Assets	**$88,880,000**	**$111,418,000**	**$117,308,273**
Total Deposits	$78,484,000	$96,632,000	$99,085,440
Other Liabilities	$2,670,000	$3,694,000	$1,382,203
Total Equity	$7,726,000	$11,092,000	$16,840,631
Total Liabilities and Equity	**$88,880,000**	**$111,418,000**	**$117,308,273**

While the bank was financed conservatively, it still earned solid returns in spite of this. This means that management must have run the business efficiently in order to make up for the fact that the assets were yielding lower returns. Additionally, the bank could become more aggressive with its assets once it was a part of Berkshire. The additional capital within Berkshire, as well as the more diversified earning power, could add layers of protection to help the bank through potential future difficulties.

With the bank being conservatively financed, managers must have been able to sleep well at night. Even if deposits experienced withdrawals and loans performed poorly, the bank would have options to remain in business over the long term. With the ability to look forward, we can see that the bank was much more conservative than it needed to be. Deposits kept growing consistently, going from $78.5 million in 1960, to $96.6 million in 1964, to $99.1 million in 1968. The performance of the loans continued to improve throughout the decade. However, there is nothing wrong with a bank being cautious and conservatively financed. Banks are leveraged institutions, and with financial leverage comes risk. This risk must be balanced with the fiduciary responsibility brought on with safeguarding the money of depositors. Banks also are supported by the FDIC who guarantees the safety of deposits. The support of the FDIC is a privilege that shouldn't be taken for granted by banking institutions.

The bank's loans performed well in the 1960's leading up to Berkshire's acquisition. The average amount of loans outstanding for Illinois National was $51.6 million from 1960 to 1968, while the total net loss on loans over the same period was just $202,136. This means that Illinois National had average net losses on loans of 0.04% during the period. There were some years with relatively high losses in the 1940's though. The bank experienced net losses on loans outstanding of 3.35% and 3.10% in 1943[33] and 1947, respectively.[34] While just looking at a few of these years may make it difficult to judge the lending ability of the bank, the loan portfolio had solid performance over the long term. There will always be some volatility in the performance of any company though.

	1960	1964	1968	1960 - 1968 Average
Loans	$39,147,000	$53,475,000	$46,995,450	$51,627,606
Net Losses (Recoveries)	$204,627	-$207,894	$90,544	$22,460
Net losses as a % of Loans	0.52%	-0.39%	0.19%	0.04%

	1960	1964	1968
Interest income	$2,917,124	$3,968,722	$5,702,018
Earning Assets	$74,908,000	$90,952,000	$91,721,346
Income from Earning Assets	3.9%	4.4%	6.2%
Interest Expense	$499,740	$804,275	$1,495,698
Interest Bearing Liabilities	$78,484,000	$96,632,000	$99,085,440
Cost of Funding	0.6%	0.8%	1.5%
Net Interest Margin	3.3%	3.6%	4.7%

The expenses involved with running a bank like Illinois National are not too complicated. Banks take in deposits from customers, and usually have to pay interest on these deposits. Demand deposits, or checking accounts, would be an exception as these are typically noninterest bearing due to their short-term nature. The bank would need an office where customers can conduct business, furniture and equipment within the office, and employees to run the bank. The bank uses customers' deposits to make loans, and a portion of these loans will never be repaid. This means that losses on loans are a regular operating expense as well.

It is difficult for banks to differentiate themselves in terms of interest expense. Switching banks is a hassle for people, but if the bank next door is going to consistently offer higher interest rates on deposits, then eventually that bank will steal some customers. Other expenses are much more manageable, and can vary greatly between banks. A lean and efficient company could operate with lower relative salaries and employee benefits than bloated competitors, but quality employees still need to be compensated fairly. The area in which Illinois National was really able to develop its efficiencies was in overhead costs such as occupancy, maintenance, and other operating expenses.

Due to the banking laws in their state, Illinois National could only conduct business at one branch office. Even though Illinois National wasn't expanding in terms of physical locations, the company experienced consistent growth in terms of loans and deposits. This meant that the bank was growing its income faster than its overhead costs. In the 25 year period leading up to the acquisition, Illinois National experienced a compound annual growth rate[35] of 10.1% in terms of total operating income. At the same time, operating expenses grew at a slightly slower rate, leading to net income growth of 11.5%.[36]

Illinois National was unique in terms of their deposits per branch. At the time of the Berkshire acquisition, the bank had deposits of $99.1 million all at a single location. This figure would be approximately $727.9 million[37] in 2019 adjusted for inflation, which is an incredibly high amount of deposits per branch. In 2019, very few banks had deposits greater than $100 million per branch. Two of the most efficient U.S. banks, Bank of America and Cullen/Frost, had deposits per branch of $333.7 million[38] and $194.6 million[39] at the end of 2019, respectively. Wells Fargo, another well-run bank, had deposits per branch of $178.7 million.[40] These three banks enjoy economies of scale, and benefit from software and online banking that were difficult to imagine in the 1960's. Even with these advantages, they still trail the deposits per branch achieved by Illinois National in the 1960's and 1970's by a wide margin. In 1968, Wells Fargo had deposits of $4.7 billion and hundreds of branch offices.[41] Wells Fargo would have needed to operate less than 48 branches in 1968 to match Illinois National's deposit per branch efficiency. More deposits means more assets that can earn interest. A stagnant number of physical locations means that overhead expenses should have less pressure to inflate over time. The management of Illinois National showed impressive ability in being able to continue growing deposits without expanding physical locations, especially during this time period.

The bank earned $625,064 of profits in 1960, which was only a return on assets of 0.7%. The return on equity was 8.1%. However, this improved over the ensuing years. By 1964, profits were $1.3 million, which amounted to a more respectable return on assets of 1.2% and a return on equity of 11.8%. By 1968, Illinois National reported net income of $1.7 million and a 1.4% return on assets. The return on equity decreased to 9.9% as the bank's equity grew and cash piled up on the balance sheet.

Berkshire paid $190 per share to acquire Illinois National, plus $2 per share to an investment bank for services rendered in the transaction. This valued the bank at $19.2 million in 1969. The bank earned $2 million before gains or losses on securities that year, which was a yield of 10.3% based on Berkshire's purchase price. The 10 year treasury bond yielded 7.7% at the time.[42] The business had security losses of $372,351 which led to net income of $1.6 million. Gains and losses of securities can be volatile, so it's better to judge the year-to-year performance of the bank using income before securities gains or losses. Over the long term, gains or losses of securities can be meaningful, but should be ignored in the short term when judging performance.

Once the bank became a subsidiary of Berkshire, it paid out a high percentage of its earnings as a dividend to the parent company. There was little reinvestment opportunity within Illinois National due to the state banking laws. The bank couldn't expand its reach in terms of adding more branches, so it made sense to pay out most of its profits as a dividend. Since Berkshire owned more than 80% of the bank, it did not have to pay a tax on the dividends received. This is one of the advantages of the conglomerate corporate structure that Berkshire was forming. Subsidiaries could move cash up to the parent level, and Buffett could reinvest those profits more efficiently. The bank paid out dividends of $1.2 million in 1969, and $2 million in 1970.[43] This means that Berkshire got 6.1% of its investment paid back in 1969 through dividends, and another 10.4% in 1970. So within two years, the bank paid out dividends of 16.5% of Berkshire's purchase price. The bank had paid over $25 million in dividends to Berkshire by 1980, which was more than the original purchase price.

When Berkshire initially announced the purchase of Illinois National, the company disclosed that it purchased 82% of the shares of the bank. Berkshire offered to buy out the rest of the shares at the same price. By the end of 1969, Berkshire owned 97.7% of the bank. The funding sources for this acquisition followed a similar pattern to the National Indemnity acquisition from 1967. Capital was taken out of the textile business, and the marketable securities portfolio was mostly liquidated. Berkshire also increased its debt in 1969.

The fact that Berkshire was able to fund over half of the Illinois National acquisition by liquidating its marketable securities portfolio was pretty incredible. Berkshire didn't even have a marketable securities portfolio just five years earlier. In 1968, only $5.4 million appeared on the balance sheet in terms of marketable securities because accounting rules required they be shown at cost.[44] In the notes to the financial statements, it was disclosed that the portfolio had a fair value of $11.8 million.[45] Berkshire first started investing in common stocks in 1965 after pulling capital out of textiles, and just three years later this portfolio was worth 118.1% above its cost. This capital would not have compounded anywhere close to such a high rate if it remained invested in the textile business. The Illinois National acquisition further diversified Berkshire's operations into businesses with more acceptable returns on capital.

Berkshire Hathaway[46]	1969
Net Earnings	$7,952,789
Depreciation and Amortization	$643,143
Loss on Liquidation or Retirement of Textile Properties	$228,788
Equity in Undistributed Earnings of Unconsolidated Subsidiaries	-$2,649,829
Funds Derived from Operations	**$6,174,891**
Long Term Debt Financing	$6,000,000
Proceeds from Sale of Textile Properties	$240,865
Decrease in Working Capital	$8,877,815
Funds Provided	**$21,293,571**
Investment in Unconsolidated Subsidiaries	$20,039,555
Repayment of Long-Term Debt	$750,000
Additions to Property and Equipment	$264,016
Purchase of Treasury Stock	$240,000
Funds Used	**$21,293,571**

In 1969, Berkshire earned $8 million. The parent company received cash flows of $6.2 million from operations that year though, as $2.6 million was earned at the unconsolidated subsidiaries. National Indemnity, one of the unconsolidated subsidiaries, retained all of its earnings. This means that Berkshire, as the parent company, never received the earnings of National Indemnity in cash. Berkshire took its own cash flow from operations, along with cash raised from the sale of textile properties and a decrease in working capital, to fund the Illinois National acquisition. The decrease in working capital mostly came from the sale of marketable securities, which was a current asset. Inventory and receivables also decreased in 1969.

"Unusually high liquidity is maintained with obligations of the U.S. Government and its agencies, all due within one year, at yearend amounting to about 75% of demand deposits."
-Warren Buffett's 1975 Letter to Berkshire Hathaway Shareholders

Although Illinois National operated conservatively prior to the acquisition, the bank became even more conservative as a subsidiary of Berkshire. In 1968, the year before Berkshire's acquisition, demand deposits made up 58.2% of the total deposits of Illinois National.[47] Demand deposits decreased to 40.6% of the total five years later[48], and was down to just 31.4% 10 years later.[49] Demand deposits typically have little to no restrictions for customers in terms of withdrawals. Time deposits, on the other hand, had to remain deposited for a specific period of time. This makes time deposits a safer source of funding for banks. However, time deposits are more costly as higher interest rates must be paid on them.

	1968	1973	1978
Demand Deposits	$57,676,992	$55,716,465	$58,132,746
As %	58.2%	40.6%	31.4%
Time Deposits	$41,408,448	$81,450,028	$127,001,647
As %	41.8%	59.4%	68.6%
Total Deposits	**$99,085,440**	**$137,166,493**	**$185,134,393**
As %	**100.0%**	**100.0%**	**100.0%**

In addition to conservative sources of funds on the liability side, Illinois National was conservative on the asset side as well. Cash and bonds consistently made up over half of the bank's assets. The bonds were made up of U.S. government securities and obligations of states and political subdivisions. These were relatively safe bonds. Loans accounted for 40.1% of assets in 1968[50], but fell to 35.3% of assets by 1978.[51] Demand deposits were more than covered by cash and these low-risk bonds. In 1968, cash and bonds made up 117.8% of the demand deposit balance. A decade later, the amount of cash and bonds was 2.2 times higher than the demand deposit balance.

	1968	1973	1978
Cash	$23,244,160	$26,683,653	$20,231,765
U.S. Treasury Securities	$26,922,563	$804,781	$565,983
U.S. Government Agencies	-	$10,550,049	$42,372,484
Obligations of States and Political Subdivisions	$17,803,334	$47,712,563	$63,576,532
Total Cash and Bonds	**$67,970,057**	**$85,751,046**	**$126,746,764**

	1968	1973	1978
Total Cash and Bonds	57.9%	54.1%	58.7%
Loans	40.1%	41.7%	35.3%
Other Assets	2.0%	4.2%	6.0%
Total Assets	**100.0%**	**100.0%**	**100.0%**

	1968	1973	1978
Cash and Bonds	$67,970,057	$85,751,046	$126,746,764
Demand Deposits	$57,676,992	$55,716,465	$58,132,746
Cash and Bonds as % of Deposits	117.8%	153.9%	218.0%

Most bankers would laugh at the idea that a bank could be profitable for shareholders when operated like Illinois National. Loans typically earn the most interest income for banks, and demand deposits are paid the least amount of interest. Maximizing these two items can lead towards higher net interest margins. However, this increases financial risk. Illinois National took less risk than most competitors, and still was able to earn good returns for shareholders. From 1969 to 1978, Illinois National earned an average of 2.2% on assets and 14.7% on equity. These are good returns for any bank, but they are fantastic for one with so much excess liquidity and such little leverage.

	1968	1973	1978
Net Income	$1,660,911	$2,848,225	$4,342,972
Total Assets	$117,308,273	$158,404,334	$215,814,564
ROA	1.4%	1.8%	2.0%
Total Equity	$16,840,531	$19,239,029	$25,910,278
ROE	9.9%	14.8%	16.8%

The success of Illinois National was due to the efficiency of its operations. Over the decade that followed Berkshire's acquisition, operating earnings compounded at a growth rate of 9.3%. Deposits and loans experienced compound annual growth rates of 6.5% and 4.9%, respectively. While the business was growing, it still operated out of only one branch location. This led to noninterest expenses growing at a slower rate than operating earnings. Net occupancy expenses decreased overall throughout the decade. As a percentage of operating earnings, salaries and wages decreased from 16.5% in 1968 to 13.8% in 1978. Net occupancy expense decreased from 5% of operating earnings in 1968 to just 2% in 1978. The bank's efficiency ratio, which is the noninterest expense divided by total revenues, improved from 34.9% in 1968 to 21.8% in 1978. Management was able to consistently grow earnings while keeping down costs.

	1968	1973	1978
Operating Income	$6,490,532	$10,403,435	$15,743,647
CAGR		9.9%	9.3%
Deposits	$99,085,440	$137,166,493	$185,134,393
CAGR		6.7%	6.5%
Loans	$46,995,450	66,022,357	76,121,628
CAGR		7.0%	4.9%

Noninterest Expense	1968	1973	1978
Salaries and Wages	16.5%	14.5%	13.8%
Pension and Profit Sharing	2.1%	2.5%	0.0%
Net Occupancy Expense	5.0%	4.0%	2.0%
Equipment Rentals, Depreciation, and Maintenance	3.6%	2.4%	1.3%
Other Operating Expenses	7.7%	7.4%	4.7%
Total Noninterest Expense	34.9%	30.8%	21.8%
Total Operating Earnings	100.0%	100.0%	100.0%

Due to regulatory changes, Berkshire was no longer allowed to fully own a bank without becoming a bank holding company. Buffett was not interested in becoming a bank holding company, so he decided to spin-off the bank to shareholders. The insurance business of Berkshire already faced regulations, so it was probably unfeasible to mix in banking regulations as well. At the end of 1980, shares of the bank were distributed to Berkshire shareholders.[52]

Berkshire in the Late 1960's

Buffett first bought shares in Berkshire when the company was selling for $12.1 million in 1962. When Buffett joined the board at Berkshire in 1965, the business was selling for $20.5 million[53] while it had a book value of $22.1 million.[54] This would mean that the market value compounded at a rate of 19.3% over a three year period. The shares outstanding dropped from 1.6 million to 1 million over that time period, so the stock price grew at an even faster rate. At the high point in 1969, Berkshire was worth $42.7 million and had a book value of $43.9 million.[55] This would equate to a compound annual growth rate in market value of 19.8% from 1962 to 1969. The 1965 annual report disclosed that BPL, the partnership Buffett controlled, owned 54.3% of Berkshire as of January 21, 1966. At the time, 54.3% of Berkshire meant ownership of 552,528 shares of its stock. BPL owned 69.99% of Berkshire by April 7, 1969 as it increased its ownership of Berkshire to 712,181 shares of stock.[56] At the end of 2019, these 712,181 shares would have represented ownership of 43.8% of Berkshire and would have been worth $241.8 billion. Buffett wound down BPL at the end of 1969, and his partners received cash as well as their share of Berkshire, Blue Chip, and Diversified Retailing stock. Buffett held onto his share of the three companies.

Berkshire looked very different at the end of 1969 than it did earlier in the decade. Sales within the textile operations declined 24.1% since 1962.[57] However, Berkshire earned $8 million[58] in 1969 compared to a loss of $2.2 million in 1962. The company benefited from $3.8 million of earnings from its unconsolidated subsidiaries, most notably National Indemnity and Illinois National. Additionally, Berkshire had realized gains on investments of $3.7 million in 1969. Textiles earned less than $0.5 million after tax. Over the five year period from 1965 to 1969, marketable securities brought in almost double the income that the textile operations did. The insurance business, which had only been owned for three years, earned far more than the textile business did in five.

Segment Income[59]	Marketable Securities*	Textiles	Insurance	Banking	Total Net Income
1965	$41,737	$2,237,469	-	-	$2,279,206
1966	$166,819	$2,595,695	-	-	$2,762,514
1967	$352,068	-$1,285,171	$2,040,562	-	$1,107,459
1968	$2,528,838	-$363,201	$2,496,699	-	$4,662,336
1969	$3,833,507	$395,740	$2,115,270	$1,608,272	$7,952,789
Total	$6,922,969	$3,580,532	$6,652,531	$1,608,272	$18,764,304

*Includes dividends and gains realized outside of the insurance business

The $6.9 million in income earned from 1965 to 1969 was within the parent company's marketable securities portfolio. Gains from marketable securities that were within the insurance business were not included in this column. However, investment income accounted for a major part of the earnings from insurance. While underwriting was profitable over the period, 90.6% of the pretax earnings for National Indemnity came from investing activities. The 'Net Investment Income' line item in the following table relates to interest on bonds, as well as dividends received from stocks. The 'Realized Gains on Investments' line item was the result of gains from the sale of securities. Net investment income was the largest source of income. This makes sense, as policyholder funds were much higher than shareholders' equity over the period. Also, the gain on the sale of investments can be volatile due to timing.

Pretax Income	1967	1968	1969	Total
Net Underwriting Gain	$358,236	$561,777	-$171,302	$748,711
Net Investment Income	$1,279,364	$1,612,059	$2,025,201	$4,916,624
Realized Gains on Investments	$922,581	$974,936	$388,789	$2,286,306
Pretax Income	**$2,560,181**	**$3,148,772**	**$2,242,688**	**$7,951,641**

Pretax Income	1967	1968	1969	Total
Net Underwriting Gain	14.0%	17.8%	-7.6%	9.4%
Net Investment Income	50.0%	51.2%	90.3%	61.8%
Realized Gains on Investments	36.0%	31.0%	17.3%	28.8%
Pretax Income	**100.0%**	**100.0%**	**100.0%**	**100.0%**

Berkshire's only business in 1962 was within the textile industry. By the end of the decade, the company had operations in the insurance, banking, and publishing industries. The shares outstanding for Berkshire declined by 39.1% over this period, so continuing shareholders owned a higher percentage of the company in 1969 than earlier in the decade. Not only were earnings coming from much more diversified sources, but from businesses with better economics than the original textile business. The return on capital steadily improved for Berkshire. The return on equity went from a negative value in 1962,[60] to 8.1% in 1965,[61] and then to 18.1% in 1969.[62] So much value was created for shareholders over this period. The stock price responded accordingly, selling for between $31 and $42 per share in 1969.[63] This means that the stock price of Berkshire compounded at an annual rate of between 22.5% and 27.9% from Buffett's original purchase in 1962.

Berkshire's profits in 1969 were $8 million, or 51.8% of the market value Berkshire had at the low point of 1965.

	1962	1965	1969
Net Income	-$2,151,256	$1,979,206	$7,952,789
Total Equity	$32,463,701	$24,520,114	$43,918,060
Return on Equity	-6.6%	8.1%	18.1%

Although the return on equity looks attractive in 1969, it is slightly misleading. Berkshire recognized a meaningful gain on the sale of investments in 1969.[64] This realized gain was the result of multiple years of investment, but the gain was only recognized in 1969 due to accounting rules. Due to this, 1969 is slightly overstated while the preceding few years are slightly understated. While this may distort the level of normalized earning power in a single year, the realized gain on sale of investments was truly a part of Berkshire's operations over the long term. All of the gains from investments would be meaningful for shareholders over the decades.

Through BPL, Buffett invested in a company worth $12.1 million that had equity in textile assets on the books for $32.5 million. Seven years later, without injecting any additional equity capital into the business, this investment was worth $42.7 million and had equity in insurance, banking, publishing, and textile assets on the books for $43.9 million. National Indemnity and Illinois National would continue to produce cash for Buffett to reinvest, and those investments would produce even more cash for Buffett to reinvest. Buffett had created a beautiful compounding machine.

Assets	Cash	Marketable Securities*	Textiles	Insurance and Banking	Total Assets
1964	$920,089	-	$26,966,957	-	$27,887,046
1965	$775,504	$2,900,000	$24,546,883	-	$28,222,387
1966	$628,721	$5,445,795	$26,821,662	-	$32,896,178
1967	$466,275	$3,856,517	$24,203,312	$9,468,865	$37,994,969
1968	$1,605,600	$5,421,394	$23,957,991	$12,754,985	$43,739,970
1969	$1,792,835	$294,165	$19,025,168	$35,444,369	$56,556,537

% of Total Assets	Cash	Marketable Securities*	Textiles	Insurance and Banking	Total Assets
1964	3.3%	-	96.7%	-	100.0%
1965	2.7%	10.3%	87.0%	-	100.0%
1966	1.9%	16.6%	81.5%	-	100.0%
1967	1.2%	10.2%	63.7%	24.9%	100.0%
1968	3.7%	12.4%	54.8%	29.2%	100.0%
1969	3.2%	0.5%	33.6%	62.7%	100.0%

*At cost

66

VII. The Expansion
1970's

Through the early 1970's, Berkshire continued to expand both internally and through acquisitions. All of this expansion occurred while the traditional textile operation declined. Sales from textiles amounted to $33.4 million[1] in 1973, down 32.2% since 1965 and 17.4% below the level of 1969.[2] While the textile business was slowly dying, insurance was enjoying solid growth. Net premiums written by the insurance businesses increased 75% from 1969 to 1973 for a compound annual growth rate of 15%.[3] As the following table[4] shows, premiums fluctuated quite a bit within some of the individual insurance segments. The "Specialized Auto, General Liability, and Other" segment, which was the traditional National Indemnity business, grew 83.6% from 1969 to 1971. From 1971 to 1973 this segment decreased by 40.1%.

Berkshire entered the insurance business in 1967 through the acquisition of National Indemnity. At that time, National Indemnity had net written premiums of $22 million and made up 100% of Berkshire's total insurance premium volume.[5] By 1973, net premiums written increased to $50.4 million and came from more diversified sources. The traditional National Indemnity segment accounted for 56.8% of net written premiums, while the remainder came from the 'Reinsurance', 'Urban Auto', and 'Home State' segments. The 'Reinsurance' and 'Home State' segments were businesses that were formed internally, while 'Urban Auto' originated through the Home and Automobile Insurance Company acquisition.

	1969	1970	1971	1972	1973
National Indemnity*	$26,034,000	$37,820,000	$47,794,000	$35,354,000	$28,617,000
Reinsurance	$2,742,000	$7,017,000	$14,953,000	$11,436,000	$10,184,000
Urban Auto	-	-	$2,040,000	$6,874,000	$6,571,000
Home State	-	$249,000	$1,668,000	$4,286,000	$5,000,000
Total	**$28,776,000**	**$45,086,000**	**$66,455,000**	**$57,950,000**	**$50,372,000**

68

	1969	1970	1971	1972	1973
National Indemnity*	90.5%	83.9%	71.9%	61.0%	56.8%
Reinsurance	9.5%	15.6%	22.5%	19.7%	20.2%
Urban Auto	-	-	3.1%	11.9%	13.0%
Home State	-	0.6%	2.5%	7.4%	9.9%
Total	100.0%	100.0%	100.0%	100.0%	100.0%

*Referred to as "Specialized Auto, General Liability, and Other" in 1973 Annual Report

Capital invested within the textile operations continued to decrease through the early 1970's. Beginning in 1973, Berkshire started consolidating the insurance subsidiaries within the reported financial statements in the annual report.[6] This makes a year-over-year comparison of the balance sheet a little more confusing at first glance. However, the company provided a breakdown of certain assets in the notes. The main assets tied up in the textile business were receivables, inventories, and property, plant, and equipment. Receivables in the textile operation went from $7.4 million[7] in 1965, to $3.9 million[8] in 1970, to $4.4 million[9] at the end of 1974. Inventory was $10.3 million in 1965 before dropping to $8.5 million in 1970 and $6 million in 1974. Property, plant, and equipment amounted to $6.6 million in 1965, but decreased to $2.5 million and $2.3 million in 1970 and 1974, respectively. The reduction in capital within the textile operation was partially due to declining sales. A business needs less inventory when conducting a lower level of volume. However, management intentionally pursued other business ventures as opposed to pouring more money into textiles.

Textile Business	1965	1970	1974
Receivables	$7,422,726	$3,916,332	$4,377,918
Inventory	$10,277,178	$8,471,798	$5,999,552
PPE	$6,617,447	$2,493,775	$2,332,879
Total	$24,317,351	$14,881,905	$12,710,349

"Further redeployment of capital from the textile business to the insurance businesses occurred in 1970 and 1971; these funds were supplemented with additional borrowed money. These capital moves enabled the insurance companies to absorb additional volume of profitable underwritings at a time when the insurance industry was generally strained for capacity."
– 1971 Berkshire Hathaway Annual Report

Through the decades, Berkshire has avoided the use of large amounts of debt. This doesn't mean that debt was never used though. Berkshire paid off all its debt in 1965 when Buffett took control of the company.[10] Berkshire had $2.6 million in debt in 1967 after acquiring National Indemnity.[11] In 1969, $7.4 million of debt was on the balance sheet in order to help fund the acquisition of the Illinois National Bank of Rockford.[12] Debt grew to $20.6 million in 1973 as additional capital was needed to fund the expansion of the insurance businesses.[13] Berkshire was opportunistic in terms of its financial structure, which has been a common theme for the company over its history. Some companies target specific debt to equity ratios, but that has never been Berkshire's style.

In 1973, Berkshire issued $20 million of debt at 8% interest. The debt became due 20 years later in 1993.[14] This means that Berkshire would have to pay $1.6 million of interest each year. Starting in 1979, Berkshire would have to start paying $1.1 million of the principal annually to pay off the debt. The company also had $598,540 of debt remaining on its debentures due in 1987. This total amount of leverage seems conservative from multiple different angles. Berkshire had equity of $81.2 million in 1973, which means that debt was 25.4% of equity. On the flip side, total assets were $196.1 million in 1973, or 2.4 times higher than equity that year.[15] The company reported net income of $12.9 million in 1973. Its earnings before interest and taxes[16] amounted to $17.8 million, which was 11.2 times higher than Berkshire's annual interest expense.[17] While this was more leverage than Berkshire had taken on in previous years, it still seemed like a prudent level of debt given the opportunities for growth.

> "In retrospect, it is clear that significantly higher, though still conventional, leverage ratios at Berkshire would have produced considerably better returns on equity than the 23.8% we have actually averaged. Even in 1965, perhaps we could have judged there to be a 99% probability that higher leverage would lead to nothing but good. Correspondingly, we might have seen only a 1% chance that some shock factor, external or internal, would cause a conventional debt ratio to produce a result falling somewhere between temporary anguish and default... We wouldn't have liked those 99:1 odds – and never will."
> – Warren Buffett's 1989 Letter to Berkshire Hathaway Shareholders

Home and Automobile Insurance Company

Berkshire acquired the Home and Automobile Insurance Company for about $2 million on September 30, 1971.[18] Home and Auto was founded in 1959 by Victor Raab, and was based in Chicago.[19] The business wrote premiums of $7.5 million at the time.[20] This means that Berkshire paid a price to sales ratio of 0.27 for Home and Auto. National Indemnity, on the other hand, was acquired for a price to sales ratio of 0.39.[21] Berkshire recorded goodwill of under $400,000 on the transaction.[22] This means that Berkshire paid around 20% above book value based on the $2 million purchase price.

Up until the acquisition, Home and Auto focused its underwriting efforts in the Chicago area. Rates were set based on the loss expectancy in its one distinct area. Following the acquisition by Berkshire, the business decided to expand into new territories. Home and Auto started doing business in Miami in 1973.[23]

> "While Vic has multiplied the original equity of Home & Auto many times since its founding, his ideas and talents have always been circumscribed by his capital base. We have added capital funds to the company, which will enable it to establish branch operations extending its highly-concentrated and on-the-spot marketing and claims approach to other densely populated areas. "
> –Warren Buffett's 1971 Letter to Berkshire Hathaway Shareholders

Due to the track record developed by Home and Auto, Berkshire attempted to expand the business geographically. Management hoped that they could take this business model and apply it to more urban areas around the country. In 1973, Miami accounted for less than 20% of Home and Auto's premiums.[24] By 1974, the Miami business reached 25%, or $1.7 million of premiums.[25] Unfortunately, Berkshire quickly realized that there were issues with the expansion efforts.

Berkshire was attracted to Home and Auto due to its history of profitable underwriting. However, in 1973 the business had an adjusted pretax underwriting loss of $878,000.[26] In 1974, this underwriting loss reached $2.2 million,[27] mostly due to a $1.6 million underwriting loss coming from the Miami operation.[28] After producing an underwriting loss about equal to the premium volume, the Miami operation was quickly discontinued. Rates were increased in Chicago, which had the effect of reducing the volume in its traditional business as well. After earning premiums of $6.6 million in 1974, Home and Auto earned premiums of $3.1 million and $3.5 million in 1975 and 1976, respectively.[29]

After the painful experience of the attempted expansion, Berkshire decided to replace the management of Home and Auto. Whenever Home and Auto was mentioned in annual reports going forward, Chicago was the only area mentioned. It appears that Home and Auto was able to stay out of trouble after going back to specializing in one area. Home and Auto

72

produced an underwriting loss of $848,000 in 1975, but this dropped to a loss of just $61,000 in 1976.[30] The results for Home and Auto were not broken out individually in the annual reports after 1976. By this time, the business was no longer a material portion of the overall insurance group at Berkshire. In the 1985 annual report, Home and Auto was listed within the company's discontinued operations.[31]

Home and Auto[32]	1973[33]	1974	1975	1976
Premiums Written	$6,571,000	$6,613,000	$3,072,000	$3,463,000
Premium Growth		0.6%	-53.5%	12.7%
Underwriting Gain (Loss)	-$878,000	-$2,183,000	-$848,000	-$61,000

Home State Operations

"During 1970 National Indemnity Company formed a subsidiary insurance company, Cornhusker Casualty Company. National Indemnity owns 100% of the outstanding stock of Cornhusker Casualty Company..."
– 1970 Berkshire Hathaway Annual Report

Berkshire expanded through the years by making numerous acquisitions. In the insurance field, National Indemnity and Home and Auto are two acquisitions that have already been discussed. However, Berkshire was entrepreneurial as well. The Home State companies were formed internally throughout the 1970's. The business strategy was to create independent companies each focusing on one state, attempting to provide the service of a small, local company with the resources of a larger organization. The companies gained business through hundreds of independent agents.

Cornhusker Casualty, started in 1970, was the first Home State company formed.[34] The following year, the company expanded to Minnesota, forming

73

Lakeland Fire & Casualty Company. Texas United Insurance was next, followed by operations in Iowa, Kansas, and Colorado. The Home State operations grew from $249,000 of premiums written in 1970 to $5.4 million in 1974.[35] Volume expanded rapidly in the mid 1970's, as $8.1 million and $14.6 million of premiums were written in 1975 and 1976, respectively.[36]

Home State	1970	1975	1980	1985
Premiums*	$249,000	$8,148,000	$43,089,000	$43,208,000
Premium Growth		3172.3%	428.8%	0.3%
Underwriting Gain (Loss)		-$877,000	-$5,294,000	-$2,791,000

*The Annual Report disclosed premiums written in 1970 and 1975, but disclosed premiums earned in 1980 and 1985 for the Home State operations.

Much like the situation with Home and Auto, the expansion of the Home State operations brought about some difficulties. While some premium growth was achieved, profitability was an issue. By the end of 1975, five years after the business began, only the Cornhusker Casualty Company had been able to produce an underwriting profit in any single year. Texas United Insurance was formed in 1972, but by the end of 1973 Berkshire was already reducing its business there until better underwriting could be achieved. Eventually, the Home State companies that were unprofitable were shut down. The business in Iowa was discontinued in 1980, while Lakeland Fire & Casualty in Minnesota was terminated in 1982. Texas United Insurance was presumably shut down around 1984, as it was no longer listed as part of the Home State operations at that time. The Home State businesses in Nebraska, Kansas, and Colorado remained intact by the end of 1985.

Overall, the Home State Operations produced an underwriting loss in almost all years from 1970 to 1985. Some individual Home State companies were able to underwrite profitably though, and all of these businesses produced investment income as well. The operations that were discontinued weighed down the overall results in certain years. Additionally, the 10 year

74

treasury bond rose to 12.8% in 1980.[37] This means that it cost the U.S. Government 12.8% to borrow money that year. A prudent business manager should always strive for profitable underwriting, but the high interest rates at the time make this underwriting performance appear less problematic.

Reinsurance

Shortly after Berkshire acquired National Indemnity, the company created a reinsurance division. Reinsurance is a business in which one insurance company sells a policy to a different insurance company. A company might buy reinsurance in order to reduce its overall financial risk, or to limit exposure to certain catastrophes. If a company realizes they are under reserved and have taken on too much operating leverage, then it makes sense for another company with excess capital to step in and accept some of the risk. Additionally, reinsurance can help an insurance company diversify its business. If an insurance policy is too large for one company, it can keep a portion of the policy and take out reinsurance on the rest. The reinsurance business made sense for Berkshire because of its capital strength, the investment ability of its managers, and its willingness to accept volatile results.

Since Berkshire generated high returns on equity and retained its earnings, the company was overflowing with capital. The total equity of the business was growing at a fast rate, giving Berkshire the ability to take on an increasing amount of insurance volume. It is important for a reinsurer to have a strong balance sheet like Berkshire's. If a hurricane or other natural catastrophe hits, the entire industry could face a period of high losses. A reinsurance policy would be needed the most during the tough times. A reinsurer will not have long term success if its existence is called into question every time there is a difficult period within the industry. If a reinsurer goes bankrupt, they will obviously be unable to honor all of their outstanding liabilities. A company who bought reinsurance from a failed reinsurer could find out they never actually had protection at all. Over time, the amount of capital at Berkshire, combined with the diversified stream of earnings from outside the insurance industry, gave Berkshire a competitive advantage in the reinsurance field.

The reinsurance industry looked attractive to Berkshire because it usually produced large amounts of float that could earn investment income. Certain types of reinsurance have long durations, meaning that Berkshire would have more time to earn a return on policyholder funds. With Buffett managing the investments at Berkshire, this type of float would be valuable.

Berkshire's focus on the long term provided for another competitive advantage in the reinsurance industry. Berkshire proved numerous times that it was not concerned with the level of net income it produced in a single year. This indifference was shown through its investment portfolio allocation, as well as in its lack of communication with Wall Street analysts. For example, the winners within the marketable securities portfolio at Berkshire could have been sold in order to book a higher profit in any given year. The losers could have been kept unrealized, avoiding a loss from having to be reported. This does not help the long term shareholder whatsoever. Additionally, Berkshire's share of the net income of its marketable securities did not appear on the income statement due to the cost method of accounting. Instead, Berkshire could have invested in only wholly-owned businesses and had all of the net income flow through to Berkshire's own income statement. Berkshire did not make investment decisions based on the accounting presentation. Most companies make quarterly earnings projections, and management puts pressure on employees to follow through on these projections. A company worrying about next quarter's earnings might not be willing to accept large reinsurance premiums, as the results can swing in a major way quarter-to-quarter. Berkshire never gave earnings projections, and never had quarterly earnings calls with Wall Street analysts. This is the proper way to manage a business.

The reinsurance division of Berkshire began at the end of 1969, and it earned premiums of $7 million the following year.[38] Over the next 10 years, reinsurance premiums grew at a compound annual growth rate of 17%. In the five year period from 1975 to 1980, premiums compounded at a rate of 27.9% per year. However, the level of premiums dropped significantly from 1980 to 1985 as underwriting became highly unprofitable. The reinsurance segment at Berkshire had an underwriting loss of $19.7 million in 1985, while premiums only registered at $12.6 million.[39] While the long duration of reinsurance is beneficial in terms of investing the float, underwriting problems can arise that were years in the making.

Reinsurance	1970	1975	1980	1985
Premiums	$7,017,000	$9,894,000	$33,804,000	$12,616,000
Premium Growth		41.0%	241.7%	-62.7%
Underwriting Gain (Loss)		-$2,194,000	-$233,000	-$19,712,000

Even with all the competitive advantages possessed by Berkshire, the company still struggled in some years due to the industry dynamics. Competition is tough within the insurance industry, and this is especially the case within the reinsurance industry. The barriers to entry are almost nonexistent. A reinsurance business can be formed if you have capital and are willing to make a promise to pay claims at a much later date. Once the promise is made and the policy has been written, then the reinsurance company receives cash up front. The act of receiving cash first and promising to pay expenses later can cause new entrants to rush into the industry, especially if the overall industry was profitable in the recent past.

For an insurance company to be successful over the long term, it must be willing to reduce business in a major way when the underwriting would be unprofitable. The period from 1980 to 1985 shows that Berkshire was willing to scale back its business when needed. Reinsurance premiums declined 62.7% from 1980 to 1985. For some businesses, this deterioration in sales would be unbearable. For example, a company with high overhead expenses and operations exclusively in the reinsurance industry might feel compelled to find business to underwrite no matter what the cost. This type of underwriting will eventually come back to haunt any insurer. Luckily for shareholders, Berkshire had the ability and willingness to deny unprofitable business. Although underwriting can never be perfect and losses will still occur, Berkshire was at least generally able to stay out of trouble.

Government Employees Insurance Company

The Government Employees Insurance Company, also known as GEICO, became a major contributor to Berkshire's insurance operations during the 1970's. Buffett's association with GEICO goes back many decades. In December 1951, he published a report on the company titled "The Security I Like Best".[40] During that year, the 20 year old Buffett personally invested over half of his net worth into the company.[41] Buffett invested $10,282 into GEICO at just under $30 per share. This stock price gave the whole company a market valuation of about $7.3 million. Buffett sold his GEICO shares the following year after the stock price increased nicely. GEICO did quite well in the years that followed though.

At the end of 1973, GEICO had just completed 28 straight years of underwriting profits.[42] The market value of the company went over $1 billion during the year, or 142 times higher than when Buffett published his article on the company.[43] His $10,282 investment would have been worth about $1.3 million 20 years later, compounding at a rate above 27% per year.[44] Buffett's portfolio did just fine though over this period even without GEICO. BPL, the investment partnership he managed, compounded at a rate of 29.5% from 1957 to 1969.[45] The stock price of Berkshire compounded at 20.3% annually from 1965 to 2019.[46]

The cost structure of GEICO is what gave the company a competitive advantage. GEICO did not use insurance agents as almost all insurers did in those days. The company marketed directly to the consumer, mostly through the mail. The insurance industry measures profitability based on a combined ratio. The combined ratio is made up of a loss ratio and an expense ratio. Basically, the loss ratio represents the loss that year on insurance policies, while the expense ratio represents the overhead costs of running the business. GEICO's distribution method of going direct to the customer allowed the company to consistently have among the lowest expense ratios in the industry. As of 1975, GEICO's expense ratio had not exceeded 16.5% for 30 years. For a few decades leading up to this period, the property and casualty industry as a whole averaged an expense ratio of 36.9% for stock companies.[47] State Farm and Allstate, two of the largest property and casualty insurance companies at the time, reported an auto liability expense ratio of 18.3% and 24.1%, respectively.[48] A lower cost structure meant that GEICO could afford to charge customers lower rates while still earning a higher profit margin than most competitors.

Although GEICO's distribution method provided a clear advantage in terms of cost structure, few companies copied the business model. The United Services Automobile Association, or USAA, operated a similar business model focusing on members of the military. GEICO's founder, Leo Goodwin Sr., actually worked for USAA first before starting his company focusing on government employees. However, most insurance companies continued to rely on insurance agents instead of the direct marketing approach. Many of the established firms had vast networks of insurance agents already in place. It would have been difficult for these firms to abandon their agents. Companies spent decades marketing, both internally and externally, how their agents would provide better service than the competition. After committing so much time and effort to a specific business model, not many people would be willing to change their ways. New entrants to the insurance field would have a difficult time competing with GEICO as well. GEICO was founded in 1936, and had slowly been building up its brand name over the decades. The unique direct mail distribution system also presented challenges in terms of managing claims and providing service to customers. GEICO had decades of experience in efficiently handling its back office functions. Scaling up a start up company to GEICO's size while maintaining both an expense ratio below 16.5% and high quality service would not be an easy task.

Although GEICO enjoyed many advantages, the business was almost ruined in the mid 1970's. The company underpriced its policies at a time when it had too much operating leverage. This led to huge losses, nearly wiping out the shareholders. On the verge of bankruptcy, Buffett stepped in and invested in GEICO once again.

	1973	1974
Premiums Written	$534,219,554	$565,226,189
Statutory Surplus	$130,703,428	$103,048,706
Ratio	4.09	5.49

The ratio of premiums written to policyholder surplus is one indicator of financial strength for an insurer. A higher ratio means more operating leverage for the company, and therefore higher risk. A company with a lower ratio has the ability to absorb more underwriting losses. GEICO usually operated with a higher ratio than the industry average because it had such a consistent history of profitability. On a statutory basis, the ratio for GEICO was 4.09 and 5.49 in 1973 and 1974, respectively.[49] The property and casualty industry as a whole was estimated to be at 2.73 in 1974 and 1.97 in 1973.[50] Another way to view operating leverage would be in terms of reported equity using GAAP accounting. In 1974, GEICO's premiums written were 3.93 times higher than total equity. With this type of operating leverage, a combined ratio of 125.4% would wipe out the company's equity without accounting for an offsetting gain from investment activity.[51] Unfortunately for GEICO shareholders, this is just about what happened in 1975.

After 28 years of underwriting profits, GEICO reported a loss from underwriting of $5.9 million in 1974. The company's combined ratio was 101.2% for the year.[52] Due to its investment income, the business still earned profits of $25.1 million for the year.[53] This amounted to a return on equity of 17.5%.[54] The company paid out $14.2 million in dividends,[55] which the company would soon wish it would have kept on the balance sheet. GEICO's

80

underwriting loss coincided with a general stock market decline. The company ended 1974 with an unrealized loss on investments of $42.3 million, $33 million worse than the previous year.[56] This decline in value of investments reduced GEICO's equity value at a time when the company needed a strong capital base.

GEICO reported a devastating underwriting loss of $190.9 million in 1975. This translated to a net loss of $126.5 million after accounting for investment income and an income tax benefit.[57] Entering into 1975, GEICO only had retained earnings of $71.6 million after consistently paying out a dividend over the years. GEICO began the year with only $143.7 million in total equity, so there were major questions regarding GEICO's solvency going forward.[58] The ratio of premiums written to policyholder surplus increased to an unfeasible 13.4 in 1975.[59] Insurance regulators would not allow GEICO to remain in business unless capital was added and liabilities were reduced. Shareholders of GEICO saw their stock decline 96.4% from $58.88 per share[60] in 1973 to $2.13 per share in 1976.[61] The incredible amount of wealth that GEICO created over the decades had vanished in a short period of time.

While GEICO was going through this turmoil, it was unclear whether or not the firm would survive. However, the company's cost structure, its main competitive advantage, remained intact. GEICO reported a combined ratio of 124.2% in 1975, but the damage was caused by the loss ratio. The expense ratio was excellent at 14.4%, while the loss ratio amounted to a devastating 109.8%.[62] As long as GEICO could survive and improve underwriting results, its expense ratio would still be an important competitive advantage.

In order to survive, GEICO needed to raise capital, scale back its business, and focus on profitability. It was able to secure reinsurance from industry participants, which helped reduce the capital burden that the company was facing. GEICO also sold $75 million worth of preferred stock in the market to increase capital.[63] GEICO reduced the scale of its business, as all marketing programs were suspended in 1976. Most of its sales offices were closed that year as well.[64] Net premiums written decreased 30.7% after

81

accounting for reinsurance ceded. GEICO still had an underwriting loss of $60.2 million in 1976, but improvements were being made.[65] GEICO reported a net loss of $26.4 million in the first quarter of 1976, but was profitable in the second half of the year. The company reported net income of $5.8 million and $8 million in the third and fourth quarters, respectively. The ratio of premiums written to policyholder surplus went from 17 in the first quarter to three in the fourth quarter as the company added capital. The statutory surplus grew from $38.3 million in the first quarter to $136.7 million at the end of 1976. GEICO shifted its focus away from growth to profitable underwriting.[66]

1976	Q1	Q2	Q3	Q4
Premiums Earned	$164,228,822	$167,566,267	$165,425,198	$78,181,974
Underwriting Loss	-$27,842,370	-$21,409,717	-$7,253,449	-$3,726,231
Net Investment Income	$8,829,015	$9,368,668	$10,058,373	$9,869,279
Interest Expense	-$1,068,524	-$1,066,875	-$1,065,191	-$1,063,470
Income (Taxes) Credits	-$36,347	-$36,348	-$36,347	$109,042
Realized Gains (Loss) on Securities	-$6,323,621	-$549,846	$4,140,461	$2,793,113
Net income	**-$26,441,847**	**-$13,694,118**	**$5,843,847**	**$7,981,733**

1976	Q1	Q2	Q3	Q4
Statutory Surplus	$39,274,000	$27,644,000	$35,166,000	$136,665,000
Premiums Written to Surplus Ratio	17	26	19	3

> "Your Management firmly believes that the quickest way for GEICO to return to underwriting profitability is to do what the company has traditionally done best. Therefore, GEICO is concentrating heavily on attracting and selectively underwriting high quality insurance risks primarily through direct marketing methods."
> -1976 GEICO Annual Report

Historically, GEICO focused on writing insurance to only high quality drivers. That is one of the explanations for how the company got its name. In the 1930's, the company hoped that government employees would be less risky to insure. GEICO expanded its customer base over time to more than just government employees, especially as it was trying to achieve higher rates of growth. It doesn't take much underwriting ability to know that a 16 year old boy with a fast car will tend to get into more accidents than average. Certain types of companies focus on underwriting this type of risk. It is perfectly acceptable to provide insurance to a higher risk driver as long as you charge a higher rate to compensate for the risk. This had never been GEICO's main strategy though. As the company planned to reduce business volume going forward, GEICO was recommitted to only underwriting high quality drivers. Within the insurance industry, high quality drivers would be referred to as preferred risk, as opposed to standard or nonstandard risk.

Berkshire first invested in the common stock of GEICO in 1976 at an average cost of $3.18 per share. Later that year, Berkshire also paid $9.77 per share for the preferred stock that GEICO issued. Berkshire invested $4.1 million into the common stock, and $19.4 million into the preferred stock.[67] One share of the preferred stock was convertible into two shares of common stock.[68] Following these investments, Berkshire owned 15.4% of GEICO at a cost of $23.5 million.

In 1976, Berkshire's wholly-owned insurance subsidiaries wrote $94.8 million of total premiums.[69] Berkshire's 15.4% share of GEICO's net premiums written would have been $71.4 million in 1976. Since Berkshire only owned 15.4% of GEICO, its share of GEICO's premiums were not consolidated within Berkshire's financial statements. However, if you consider Berkshire's share of GEICO's premiums as its own business segment, then it would have been the largest segment within the Berkshire Hathaway Insurance Group. The traditional National Indemnity business, which was the 'Specialized Auto, General Liability, and Other' segment, wrote $60.9 million of premiums. Reinsurance would have been the next largest segment, with $15.8 million in premiums written that year.[70] GEICO had total assets of $911.8 million[71] in 1976, so Berkshire's share would have been $140.4 million. Berkshire's total assets were $283 million in 1976. These metrics prove that Berkshire's investment in GEICO was a meaningful part of its insurance operations starting in 1976. By 1980, Berkshire's share of GEICO's premiums eclipsed that of the Berkshire Hathaway Insurance Group. Additionally, Berkshire's subsidiaries produced an underwriting profit of $6.7 million[72] in 1980, while Berkshire's share of GEICO's underwriting profit amounted to $56.8 million that year.

Premiums Written by Segment	1976	1978	1980
Traditional National Indemnity	$60,860,000	$96,126,000	$88,404,000
Workers Compensation	-	$29,893,000	$19,890,000
Reinsurance	$15,823,000	$30,160,000	$33,804,000
Urban Auto	$3,463,000		
Home State	$14,627,000	$29,894,000	$43,089,000
Total*	**$94,773,000**	**$186,073,000**	**$185,187,000**
GEICO	$463,410,475	$620,763,000	$638,621,000
Berkshire's Share of GEICO	**$71,365,213**	**$95,597,502**	**$226,710,455**

*Excludes GEICO

Underwriting Gain (Loss) by Segment	1976	1978	1980
Traditional National Indemnity	$923,000	$11,543,000	$7,395,000
Workers Compensation	-	-$3,944,000	$4,870,000
Reinsurance	-$2,374,000	-$2,443,000	-$233,000
Urban Auto	-$103,000	-	-
Home State	-$1,569,000	-$2,155,000	-$5,294,000
Total*	**-$3,123,000**	**$3,001,000**	**$6,738,000**
GEICO	-$60,231,767	$174,742,000	$160,027,000
Berkshire's Share of GEICO	**-$9,275,692**	**$26,910,268**	**$56,809,585**

*Excludes GEICO

In 1979, Berkshire purchased an additional 461,900 shares of GEICO at an average cost of $10.29 per share. By this time, Berkshire had invested $28.3 million into GEICO[73] and owned 26.8% of the company.[74] Berkshire added to its position in GEICO in 1980, buying almost 1.5 million more shares at an average cost of $12.82 per share.[75] At the end of 1980, Berkshire owned 35.5% of GEICO at a total cost of $47.1 million.[76] After returning to consistent profitability, GEICO used excess cash flow to repurchase stock. This meant that Berkshire's ownership of GEICO increased to 38% by the end of 1985.[77]

Usually, Berkshire would have accounted for a holding like GEICO as an equity method investment because Berkshire owned such a large percentage of the company. This means that Berkshire's share of GEICO's net income would have shown up on its own income statement. However, Berkshire was directed by GEICO's state insurance regulator to give up the voting power of its GEICO stock. Without voting power, Berkshire didn't have enough influence or control over GEICO to account for it as an equity method investment. This led to Berkshire accounting for GEICO as a cost method investment. Due to this, only the dividends GEICO paid to Berkshire were counted as profits within Berkshire's income statement. Over time, this accounting presentation led to Berkshire's income statement significantly understating the value GEICO had to Berkshire.

	1977	1980	1983
GEICO Net Income	$58,600,000	$60,763,000	$113,753,000
Berkshire's Share of GEICO Net Income	$9,024,400	$21,570,865	$38,221,008
Dividends Received on Common Stock	$158,046	$3,096,000	$4,932,000
Berkshire's Total Reported Net Income	**$30,393,000**	**$53,122,000**	**$112,166,000**
% Increase in Net Income if Equity Method	29.2%	34.8%	29.7%

In 1977, GEICO paid a dividend of just $0.03 per share on its common stock.[78] GEICO's dividend climbed to $0.43 per share in 1980, and $0.72 per share in 1983.[79] GEICO reported net income of $58.6 million in 1977.[80] Berkshire's share of this net income would have been $9 million, but under GAAP accounting Berkshire could only include the $158,046 in dividends it received from GEICO. Berkshire's share of GEICO's net income grew to $19 million in 1980 and $36.8 million in 1983. If the equity method of accounting was used, Berkshire's total reported net income would have been 34.8% higher in 1980, and 29.7% higher in 1983. From an accounting standpoint, the dividend seemed more valuable to Berkshire than the earnings that GEICO retained. However, this was not the case economically. Berkshire had to pay a tax on all dividends received. On the other hand, Berkshire faced no additional tax on the dollars that GEICO retained. Since GEICO was a great business with a long runway for growth, each dollar of retained earnings had the potential to compound at high rates. The accounting presentation had no impact on the intrinsic value of Berkshire.

> "In discussing the question, [Abraham Lincoln] used to liken the case to that of the boy who, when asked how many legs his calf would have if he called its tail a leg, replied, "Five," to which the prompt response was made that *calling* the tail a leg would not *make* it a leg."
> -Reminiscences of Abraham Lincoln[81]

After accounting for the dilution from the preferred stock, GEICO had a market value of $72.9 million at the low point in 1976. Just two years earlier, GEICO reported net income of $25.1 million, or 34.4% of the 1976 market value.[82] GEICO had float from insurance liabilities of $489.3 million in 1976 as well.[83] GEICO reported profits of $58.6 million in 1977, a clear sign that the company had weathered the storm.[84] The profits in 1977 were 80.4% of GEICO's market value at the low end of 1976.

GEICO	1970	1975	1980	1984
Premiums Earned	$289,243,236	$603,320,611	$653,099,000	$874,896,000
CAGR		15.8%	1.6%	7.6%
Underwriting Gain (Loss)	$4,680,686	-$190,896,022	$25,286,000	$5,809,000
Net Income	$14,191,725	-$126,456,994	$60,763,000	$131,313,000

	1970	1975	1980	1984
Loss Ratio	85.6%	109.8%	80.5%	82.1%
Expense Ratio	12.1%	14.4%	15.9%	15.6%
Combined Ratio	**97.7%**	**124.2%**	**96.4%**	**97.7%**
10 Year Treasury Bond	6.4%	8.0%	12.8%	11.5%

Although the stock price of GEICO during this time period may look like a steal with the benefit of hindsight, investors at the time were facing significant risks. It was not clear in 1975 and 1976 whether or not GEICO would survive. While GEICO was able to obtain reinsurance from industry participants, the acceptance of this deal was not guaranteed. The companies providing reinsurance competed with GEICO. These companies should have been aware of GEICO's advantages in terms of its cost structure, and might not have wanted to compete with GEICO in the future. This could have led to a lack of companies willing to provide reinsurance, and ultimately could have contributed to GEICO going out of business. Additionally, shareholders in 1975 and 1976 were facing uncertainties about the degree of upcoming dilution to the common stock. GEICO had to raise capital quickly, which can lead to a lack of negotiating power. Buying GEICO stock in the open market during the mid 1970's meant taking on both bankruptcy risk, as well as the risk of major dilution.

The underwriting ability of GEICO was also called into question during this period. At the time, it would be difficult to know how quickly GEICO would recover. A prospective investor would have to gauge whether or not the underwriting losses of the mid 1970's were likely to recur in the future. It would have been reassuring to see GEICO focusing on profitability and high quality customers, but the mid 1970's proved that a few bad years of underwriting had the potential to take down a company as great as GEICO. Any institution using financial leverage, such as a bank or insurance company, constantly faces this risk.

Berkshire had a unique position during this period, as the company was willing to provide both reinsurance and equity capital to GEICO. Berkshire's insurance companies took some of the reinsurance business GEICO offered.[85] Berkshire was willing to buy the entire amount of preferred stock GEICO was selling, but the market demand was high enough that Berkshire only obtained a portion of the offering.[86] This perspective might have helped give confidence to Berkshire regarding the investment decision, but by no means eliminated the risk involved with investing in GEICO.

Cypress Insurance Company

Berkshire purchased the Cypress Insurance Company in December 1977. Cypress was based out of Los Angeles and provided insurance for workers' compensation.[87] The business earned $12.6 million in premiums in 1977.[88] Berkshire paid $2.7 million for the business, which is a price to sale ratio of 0.21.[89] Cypress wrote premiums of $14 million in 1978.[90] At this point, Berkshire was involved in worker's compensation insurance through a branch of National Indemnity, Cypress, and through a subsidiary of Diversified Retailing named Southern Casualty.

> "On December 23, 1977, an insurance subsidiary of the Company purchased for approximately $2.7 million cash all of the outstanding capital stock of Cypress Insurance Company, South Pasadena, California."
> -1977 Berkshire Hathaway Annual Report

Little financial data is disclosed on an individual company level for Cypress following the acquisition. However, Berkshire did disclose the results of the overall workers' compensation segment in the annual reports. Berkshire had minimal volume in workers' compensation prior to 1977.

Workers' Compensation	1978	1980	1982	1984
Premiums	$29,893,000	$19,890,000	$15,951,000	$22,665,000
Premium Growth		-33.5%	-19.8%	42.1%
Underwriting Gain (Loss)	-$3,944,000	$4,870,000	$2,658,000	-$12,560,000

The workers' compensation segment of Berkshire appears to have had mixed results. There were years of excellent profitability, followed by some concerning results in 1984. However, the segment remained a fairly small portion of Berkshire's overall insurance volume during this period. The workers' compensation segment earned lower premiums than both the traditional National Indemnity business and the Home State operations throughout the period. Additionally, the reinsurance segment earned higher premiums during the period, with the exception of 1984 and 1985.

Waumbec Mills

In the mid 1970's, Berkshire made the decision to acquire another textile mill. Waumbec Mills was purchased in April 1975 for $1.7 million.[91] Berkshire had total equity of $92.9 million and total assets of $225.7 million at the time, so this was a very small acquisition relative to the overall company.[92] It is interesting to see that Buffett made another textile acquisition a decade after originally taking over Berkshire.

"In 1975, Berkshire acquired additional textile products manufacturing facilities and additionally, a textile finishing plant operating in jointly occupied facilities in Manchester, New Hampshire, by purchase of all of the outstanding capital stock of Waumbec Mills Incorporated."
-1975 Berkshire Hathaway Annual Report

Similar to the original investment in Berkshire, Waumbec was a textile mill selling below book value. The problem was that the company earned poor returns on capital, also similar to the textile operations of Berkshire. Waumbec had unused tax loss carryforwards of $2.6 million, assuming the business produced enough profit to take advantage of the tax benefit.[93]

Textile Sales	1974	1975
Berkshire	$32,592,000	$23,521,000
Waumbec	-	$9,312,000
Total	$32,592,000	$32,833,000

While total sales within the textile operations looked flat from 1974 to 1975, this was only due to the Waumbec acquisition. Textile sales declined 27.8% at Berkshire in 1975, while gross profit decreased 42.4%.[94] The Waumbec acquisition could have been an attempt to keep the textile business alive for a little while longer. The textile mills employed a large number of people in the New England area, and it would have been painful to discontinue operations. Although this may have provided a brief lifeline for the textile operation, the future was looking bleak within this business segment.

Textile Gross Profit	1974	1975
Berkshire	$5,163,000	$2,972,000
Gross Margin	15.8%	12.6%
Waumbec	-	$1,627,000
Gross Margin	-	17.5%
Total	**$5,163,000**	**$4,599,000**
Gross Margin	**15.8%**	**14.0%**

K&W Products, Inc

Berkshire acquired K&W Products in January 1976 for $2.1 million.[95] The business manufactured specialty automotive chemical products in Los Angeles, California and Bloomington, Indiana. The company was formed in the 1940's, and had a history of profitability.

While K&W was small relative to Berkshire, it still serves as an interesting contrast to the old textile operations that Berkshire still managed. The textile business produced revenue of $44.6 million[96] in 1976, which was 32.1% of the company's total revenue.[97] K&W had sales of only $2.5 million, or 1.8% of total revenues. However, K&W had far better margins than the textile business. K&W earned a gross margin of 57.6%, and a pretax profit margin of 20.5%.[98] The textile business earned a gross margin of just 9.3%

and a pretax margin of 2.6% in 1976.[99] This led to much more parity in terms of profits between the new automotive chemicals business and the textile business. Berkshire reported pretax earnings of $518,000 from K&W in 1976, while textiles earned $1.1 million. The pretax earnings of K&W amounted to 1.9% of Berkshire's total, while textiles accounted for 4.1% of the total. Even though K&W might have looked less important at first glance, the business was about as meaningful as the textile business in 1976. However, K&W was probably worth more to Berkshire since it used up far less capital.

Manufacturing Segment	Textiles	K&W Products
Sales	$44,644,000	$2,530,000
Gross Profit	$4,162,000	$1,458,000
Gross Margin	9.3%	57.6%
Pretax Income	$1,148,000	$518,000
Pretax Margin	2.6%	20.5%

Starting in 1978, Berkshire no longer reported individual financial data for K&W Products. The business was small relative to Berkshire to begin with, but became even more immaterial as Berkshire continued growing and compounding its earnings. K&W was a mature business, and probably experienced little growth. Instead, it is likely that most of K&W's cash profits were sent to Berkshire to help fuel a little bit of its expansion.

VIII. The Other Companies

Diversified Retailing Company

Diversified Retailing was formed in January 1966 when Buffett, Charlie Munger, and Sandy Gottesman teamed up to buy a department store in Baltimore named Hochschild Kohn.[1] Although the company was private, it was still required to file financial statements with the SEC following a public debt offering. This was the first major investment in which Buffett and Munger were partners. Munger would go on to become Vice President of Berkshire, and both he and Gottesman would serve on Berkshire's board of directors. This investment was initially made outside of Berkshire, and instead was made through BPL while the partnership was still in existence.

Diversified acquired Hochschild Kohn for $12 million, with half of the funding coming from equity and the other half from debt.[2] In April 1967, Diversified paid $6 million to acquire Associated Cotton Shops, later named Associated Retail Stores.[3] The Associated Retail acquisition was fully funded by debt. Combined, the acquisitions were one-third funded with equity and two-thirds debt.[4]

While Diversified reported high returns on equity in fiscal 1967 and 1968, this can mostly be attributed to the large amount of debt on the balance sheet. The return on equity[5] was 32.3% in 1967, and 24.8% in 1968.[6] If you add back the debt to the total equity figure, then the returns amount to 12.8% and 11% in 1967 and 1968, respectively. The company retained all of its earnings in both years, but that isn't surprising given the track record of Berkshire. However, Diversified specifically had dividend restrictions as part of the debt offering.

The financial statements of Diversified Retailing are a beautiful sight to see because they are untainted by mortal hands. The common stock and paid-in capital line items on the balance sheet account for all of the $6 million of equity invested by Buffett, Munger, and Gottesman. This is a firm they both created and controlled. Berkshire and Blue Chip both existed long before Buffett or Munger came around.

94

> "Shortly after purchasing Berkshire, I acquired a Baltimore department store, Hochschild Kohn, buying through a company called Diversified Retailing that later merged with Berkshire. I bought at a substantial discount from book value, the people were first-class, and the deal included some extras - unrecorded real estate values and a significant LIFO inventory cushion. How could I miss? So-o-o - three years later I was lucky to sell the business for about what I had paid. After ending our corporate marriage to Hochschild Kohn, I had memories like those of the husband in the country song, "My Wife Ran Away With My Best Friend and I Still Miss Him a Lot."
> -Warren Buffett's 1989 Letter to Berkshire Hathaway Shareholders

While the financials for 1967 and 1968 for Diversified combine the results of both retail subsidiaries, it appears that Hochschild Kohn weighed down the overall results for the company. Diversified Retailing generated an unlevered return on equity of 12.8% and 11% in 1967 and 1968, respectively. In 1968, Associated Retail earned 20% on the capital employed in the business.[7] Over the next decade, this 20% return on capital was achieved often.[8] This led to the company producing a healthy level of cash flow that could be reinvested elsewhere. Associated Retail did not grow much through the 1970's, but the cash it produced could be sent tax efficiently to the parent company for Buffett to reinvest. The company had sales of $37.5 million[9] in 1968, and this grew to $40.8 million a decade later for an 0.8% compound annual growth rate.[10]

> "Associated Retail Stores has a net worth of about $7.5 million. It is an excellent business with a strong financial position, good operating margins and a record of increasing sales and earnings in recent years."
> -December 1969 BPL Letter to Partners

Associated Retail	1977	1978	1979	1980
Sales	$41,686,000	$40,762,000	$42,709,000	$44,374,000
Net Income	$1,429,000	$1,176,000	$1,280,000	$1,169,000
Profit Margin	3.4%	2.9%	3.0%	2.6%

In 1969, Diversified Retailing decided to sell Hochschild Kohn for $11 million.[11] Diversified Retailing roughly broke even on the investment over the three year period. The company used the proceeds of the transaction to pay off some debt and invest in marketable securities. The stock of both Berkshire and Blue Chip was eventually purchased for the marketable securities portfolio of Diversified Retailing. This began linking the three companies more closely to each other. Additionally, Diversified Retailing formed an insurance company called Columbia Insurance. Columbia acquired Southern Casualty in 1974, which provided workers' compensation insurance for the forest products industry in Louisiana. The decision to sell Hochschild Kohn and move on to other businesses turned out to be a good one, as the retailer went out of business in 1984.

Blue Chip Stamps

"Trading stamps are the most successful promotional tool ever devised...They offer retailers a tangible method of rewarding customers for patronage and they offer shoppers a savings plan that grows more valuable with each stamp collected."
-Blue Chip Stamps 1969 Annual Report

Blue Chip Stamps was based in Los Angeles, California and operated a type of rewards program. Blue Chip would sell stamps to retailers, who would then issue stamps to its customers. Later, customers would redeem these stamps for products at the store. Blue Chip would be on the hook for the cost of the products whenever the stamps were redeemed. This timing difference of getting paid first and incurring expenses later created float similar to the insurance business. For Blue Chip, the float that was generated showed up on the balance sheet as a liability for unredeemed trading stamps.

> "In fiscal 1969, 66,297,000,000 Blue Chip stamps were issued by 20,000 merchants. 7,000,000 consumers redeemed 57,877,000,000 Blue Chip stamps for 15,760,000 items of merchandise."
> -Blue Chip Stamps 1969 Annual Report

The float generated by Blue Chip was substantial. In 1967, for example, the company had total equity of $23.1 million, but had total assets of over four times that amount.[12] The liability for unredeemed trading stamps was over 70% of the value of its assets that year.[13] This meant that the business needed little tangible equity in order to operate the business. This float allowed Blue Chip to enjoy the use of leverage without necessarily taking on any traditional debt.

In 1967, the vast majority of Blue Chip's assets were made up of marketable securities. Most of the marketable securities portfolio was in state and municipal bonds that year.[14] As Buffett and Munger gained control of the company, the portfolio became much more heavily weighted towards stocks. In 1968, preferred and common stocks increased to 22.8% of total assets from 14.4% the year before.[15] Buffett, through BPL, and Munger, through his Wheeler, Munger & Co. partnership, initially invested in Blue Chip in 1965.[16] Munger was on the board of directors in the late 1960's, and Buffett joined in the early 1970's.[17] By 1976, Munger was the chairman of Blue Chip.[18]

	1967	1968
Cash	3.0%	2.0%
Short-term investments	13.4%	17.8%
State and Municipal Bonds	45.5%	35.2%
Preferred and Common Stocks	14.4%	22.8%
Total Cash and Marketable Securities	**76.3%**	**77.8%**
Total Assets	**100.0%**	**100.0%**

The attractiveness of Blue Chip as an investment was almost entirely due to its ability to produce profitable float. The float created a large amount of leverage for the company, so even low margins could lead to high returns on equity. Blue Chip had a gross margin of 8.7% and 12.7% in 1967 and 1968, respectively. The profit margin of the company was 3.7% and 1.8% over the same period. The 1968 figure contains an extraordinary item in the form of a $3.7 million litigation settlement expense, but without this charge the profit margin still would have been just 5.2%. The return on equity, excluding the litigation expense, amounted to 14.8% and 20.1% in those two years. Due to the leverage obtained through the use of float, Blue Chip only earned a return on assets of 4.6% and 1.6% in 1967 and 1968, respectively.[19]

	1967	1968
Gross Margin	8.7%	12.7%
Profit Margin	3.7%	1.8%
Profit Margin w/o Litigation Expense	3.6%	5.2%
Return on Equity (ROE)	14.8%	7.1%
ROE w/o Litigation Expense	14.8%	20.1%

An important piece of Blue Chip's earnings came from the investment income on its float. In 1967, investment income made up 48.8% of pretax operating income. This figure dropped to 28.8% in 1968 as operating income increased significantly on 18.2% higher stamp revenue.[20] However, both figures are meaningful percentages of income. The success of Blue Chip as an investment would have been dependent on who was managing the investment portfolio. Buffett and Munger no longer needed to worry about this fact once they gained control of the company. As skilled investment managers took over and the portfolio was allocated more aggressively towards common stocks, you would expect Blue Chip to prosper.

Berkshire wasn't the only company controlled by Buffett that was undergoing an expansion in the 1970's. Blue Chip was on its way to becoming a conglomerate as well. Much like Berkshire, the expansion Blue Chip experienced was not due to its traditional business. Stamp service revenue decreased 25% from 1970 to 1972. Even with this drop in sales, Blue Chip had ample funds to invest due to the float from its trading stamps. The liability for unredeemed trading stamps increased 6.8% over this period, from $87.4 million to $93.4 million.[21] Additionally, Blue Chip took on some debt. In December 1968, the company received authorization to borrow up to $20.7 million of debt that was due 10 years later. The loan charged 6.5% interest. At the time, Blue Chip only borrowed $10.8 million of the loan.[22] All of these factors led to Blue Chip having plenty of liquidity that could be put to work.

In early 1972, Buffett and Munger used the firm's excess liquidity to acquire their first wholly-owned company through Blue Chip. This company was named See's Candy. In April 1977, the Buffalo Evening News was acquired as well. Over this same time period, Blue Chip acquired controlling positions in Pinkerton's, Wesco Financial, and Detroit International Bridge through the open market. By the late 1970's, Blue Chip was a diversified holding company that owned some incredible businesses.

See's Candy

See's Candy began operations in 1921 when Charles See and his mother, Mary See, opened their first candy store in Los Angeles. The company expanded over the years, particularly on the west coast. By the end of 1971, See's had 152 stores ranging from Hawaii to Texas.[23] Over the decades, See's developed a brand known for high quality products.

Blue Chip acquired 67% of See's Candy in January 1972. The company increased its ownership of See's to 99% in March 1973.[24] Blue Chip paid $35 per share, which valued See's at $35 million. The balance sheet of See's reported that the business had cash of $9.9 million with no debt.[25] This means that Blue Chip paid $25.1 million net of cash acquired.

At the time of the acquisition, See's would have looked like a consistent and profitable company. Sales had increased 13 years in a row leading up to Blue Chip's acquisition, going from $13.7 million in 1958 to $28.2 million in 1971. This is a compound annual growth rate of 5.7%. The gross margin increased from 44.6% to 54.4% over this period, while the net profit margin went from 3.8% to 8%. The business produced positive earnings in each of the previous 20 years as well. Net income compounded at a rate of 8.9% over this time period, growing from $0.4 million in 1951 to $2.4 million in 1971.[26] Across many different metrics, See's appeared to be heading in the right direction.

	1958	1962	1966	1971
Sales	$13,740,767	$17,794,514	$22,660,781	$28,210,103
Gross Margin	44.6%	51.1%	53.2%	54.4%
Net Income	$522,706	$1,176,316	$1,644,957	$2,262,071
Profit Margin	3.8%	6.6%	7.3%	8.0%

It was clear that See's did not need much capital to operate when viewing the balance sheet.[27] Cash was the largest line item on the balance sheet throughout the 1960's, making up over half of the company's assets. Property, plant, and equipment was the second largest line item on the asset side, followed by inventory. See's owned a few manufacturing plants in California, which likely made up most of the property, plant, and equipment value. The vast majority of its stores were leased, which meant that a low amount of assets were tied up in owning stores. The company had almost no receivables as well because customers paid cash in the stores at the time of purchase. The capital-light nature of the business led to See's reporting a double digit return on assets in the decade leading up to Blue Chip's acquisition. The return on assets would have looked even better if the excess cash tied up in the business was removed.

The reported return on equity consistently looked good for See's, ranging from 12.9% to 17.3% in the decade prior to the acquisition. However, the reported figures understated the returns that See's was able to generate for its owners, especially once it was a part of Blue Chip. Since See's was such a consistent and capital-light business, it did not need to keep so much cash on the balance sheet. Once the business was a part of a diversified parent company, it could either reinvest or pay out that cash. Excluding cash, the return on equity would have ranged from 35.8% to 75.5% in the decade leading up to the Blue Chip acquisition. This excellent return on equity would have been achieved without using any debt.

While See's earned high returns on the capital invested in the business, Blue Chip was paying a premium to acquire it. At the end of 1971, See's had equity of $15.3 million. Blue Chip paid $35 million to acquire the company, which was 2.3 times higher than the equity of See's. However, $9.9 million of this equity was cash. Assuming Blue Chip could take the cash out of the business, this means that See's had equity of $5.4 million net of cash. Blue Chip's net purchase price would be $25.1 million, or 4.6 times higher than See's equity net of cash. The performance of the underlying business of See's should be judged based on its return on net equity of $5.4 million, but the acquisition decision of Blue Chip's management should be judged based on the return on the net purchase price of $25.1 million. Blue Chip management

101

would be responsible for earning an adequate return on the goodwill from the acquisition.

See's earned $2.3 million in 1971, which would be an immediate yield of 9% based on Blue Chip's purchase price. This initial yield was above the 10 year treasury rate of 6% in 1971.[28] Over the previous decade, the stock price of See's compounded at a rate of 13.3% annually.[29] Due to the consistent operating history of See's, $25.1 million appeared to be an acceptable price to pay even if there was little to no growth in the business going forward.

In order to fund the See's acquisition, Blue Chip took on additional debt. The company already had $10.8 million of debt outstanding due at the end of 1978. Blue Chip added $32.7 million of debt in the form of notes payable to a bank. This left Blue Chip with a total of $43.6 million in debt in 1971 compared to the $46.4 million in equity it had.[30]

Even though stamp service revenue was decreasing for Blue Chip and the company spent $25.1 million on an acquisition, the cash and investments reported on the balance sheet went up by $25 million. This can partially be explained by the increase in debt during the 1971 fiscal year. Blue Chip borrowed $7.6 million more than the cost of the See's acquisition. There were improvements in terms of working capital as well though. Accounts receivable and inventory decreased while payables increased. The liability for unredeemed trading stamps increased as well. The additional debt in 1971 and the improvements in working capital can explain about $18.2 million of the $25 million increase in funds Blue Chip was able to invest. The remainder can partially be attributable to cash profits for the year, after subtracting out the dividends that Blue Chip paid to shareholders. Blue Chip reported net income of $4.2 million in 1971, and paid $1.2 million in dividends that year.[31]

102

Year-Over-Year Change	1972
Accounts Receivable	-$2,846,000
Inventory	-$3,010,000
Prepaid Taxes and Other Expenses	$608,000
Current Assets (Excl cash + invst)	**-$5,248,000**
Accounts Payable	$2,284,000
Income Taxes Payable	$1,237,000
Liability for Unredeemed Trading Stamps	$1,816,000
Current Liabilities (Excl Debt)	**$5,337,000**
Change in Working Capital	**-$10,585,000**

	1972
Increase in Debt	$32,711,000
-Cost of Acquisition	-$25,100,000
+Decrease in Working Capital	$10,585,000
+1972 Net Income	$4,214,000
-Dividend Paid	-$1,208,000
Total Capital Generated	**$21,202,000**

Blue Chip did not need See's to grow much in order to justify the purchase price it paid. However, See's grew like a weed following the acquisition, turning the investment into a home run for Blue Chip. In 1971, See's had total sales of $28.2 million.[32] Over the next decade, the business enjoyed double digit percentage sales growth each year. The compound annual growth rate over the decade was 14.7%. Operating profit after tax compounded at a rate of 19% per year from $2.1 million in 1972, to $11.9 million in 1982.[33]

The sales growth achieved at See's mostly came from an increase in prices. Per pound realization, which can be calculated by taking the total sales divided by the number of pounds of candy sold, increased at a rate of

9.5% compounded annually from 1972 to 1984. The number of pounds of candy sold only increased by 3.2% per year, while the number of candy stores increased by just 2.1% per year. Prices at See's increased from $1.85 per pound to $5.49 per pound over the 12 year period.[34]

	1972	1984	CAGR
Sales	$31,337,000	$135,946,000	13.0%
Number of Pounds of Candy Sold	16,954,000	24,759,000	3.2%
Number of Stores Open at Year End	167	214	2.1%
Per Pound Realization	$1.85	$5.49	9.5%

Double digit sales growth is nice, but growth from increasing prices is extra special. When a retail operation increases the number of pounds sold, management is happy. However, the business must invest more money in inventory in order to sell those extra pounds. There might be an increase in costs as well, since it could take more employees to handle the greater volume. Opening a new store can also be justified when there is demand. A new store requires an investment in fixed assets though. You also need to hire employees to run the new store. Unit sales growth, led by the number of pounds sold or from the number of stores open, ties up more money in working capital and fixed assets, and adds a layer of expenses. On the flip side, increasing prices does not directly lead to an additional investment in working capital or fixed assets. No extra employees need to be hired just because your peanut brittle costs a dollar more. The incremental profit realized from raising prices can lead to actual cash flow for the owners, as opposed to just accounting earnings.

> "For an increase in profits to be evaluated properly, it must be compared with the incremental capital investment required to produce it. On this score, See's has been astounding: The company now operates comfortably with only $25 million of net worth, which means that our beginning base of $7 million has had to be supplemented by only $18 million of reinvested earnings. Meanwhile, See's remaining pre-tax profits of $410 million were distributed to Blue Chip/Berkshire during the 20 years for these companies to deploy (after payment of taxes) in whatever way made most sense."
> -Warren Buffett's 1991 Letter to Berkshire Hathaway Shareholders

For the typical business, an increase in price leads to a decrease in demand. A more efficient competitor could step in and capture market share. Consumers might switch to a more affordable substitute product. The situation at See's was a different story. The company was able to raise prices steadily while still increasing the volume sold at its stores. One explanation for this phenomenon could be related to the company's brand. Over many decades, See's became known for quality. During World War II, sugar and other ingredients for candy were rationed. Instead of using substitute ingredients, See's decided to just sell less candy. When the quality ingredients ran out, See's closed its stores early.[35] Additionally, See's does not use preservatives in their candy, even though this limits the shelf life of their products.[36] A large portion of See's candy is purchased around the holidays. If a customer is purchasing See's products as a gift, a higher price could signal higher quality to that customer. All of this helped build the See's Candy brand into one known for quality.

The Buffalo Evening News

Blue Chip purchased the Buffalo Evening News in April 1977 for $35.5 million.[37] The News was the leading newspaper in the Buffalo area during the week. Weekday circulation of the News was more than double that of its competitor.[38] However, the News did not publish a Sunday paper at the time.

While daily papers dominated the newspaper industry early in the history of the News, eventually Sunday became the most important. This was especially the case in terms of advertising.

Edward Butler, Sr. started the Buffalo Sunday News in December 1873.[39] The circulation of the News reached 10,850 during the first year.[40] At the time, there were no other Sunday papers publishing in Buffalo. Many religious organizations were against the formation of a Sunday newspaper. Eventually, competition grew over time on Sunday. The Sunday Courier was formed in 1875, while the Sunday Express began operations in 1883. These two papers would later go on to merge and form the Courier-Express. In 1880, Butler decided to establish the Buffalo Evening News, a daily edition of the newspaper. In 1915, the News shut down their Sunday operations as the daily paper was more profitable at the time.

Buffett noticed that most cities were dominated by one newspaper. From 1920 to 1977, the number of cities in the U.S. with two major newspapers dropped from 700 down to less than 50.[41] Local businesses would pay more to advertise within the newspaper that had a higher customer base. Readers would get more useful information from a newspaper that contained more advertising because they would be able to view more classified ads, as well as learn about discounts from local retailers. Additionally, a paper with more financial resources could have a higher budget to report the news, leading to a higher quality product. The economics of the newspaper industry led to a winner-take-all situation.

Blue Chip invested $35.5 million in the News in 1977. The cost of net assets acquired exceeded their reported fair value by $1.1 million.[42] Blue Chip took out a $30 million bank loan to fund the acquisition. As a result of prepayments, the loan was only $13.5 million by 1979.[43] The News earned $1.7 million pretax[44] in 1976, or $863,008 after tax based on the 48% statutory tax rate. This would be a 2.4% after tax yield based on Blue Chip's purchase price. At first glance, this may seem like an expensive price to pay for a business. However, the profitability at the News had the potential to increase to levels that would make the purchase price look like a bargain.

The News had been privately owned for a century, and Blue Chip had the opportunity to reduce certain operating costs. For example, the News was paying higher prices than necessary for its newsprint, a raw material. Most mills offered volume discounts. The News, on the other hand, bought newsprint from many different mills to protect against the chance of a strike.[45] When Blue Chip took over the News, the company reduced the number of mills it purchased from in order to take advantage of volume discounts. The company also increased storage capacity in order to help protect against a shortage in the case of a strike at a mill. Buffett hoped to save $1.2 million in newsprint costs after renegotiating with the mills.[46] This reduction in costs would have led to a $2.9 million pretax profit in 1976, or roughly $1.5 million after tax. Blue Chip's effective yield on their purchase price would have been 4.2% under this scenario. Blue Chip ended up being successful in lowering its newsprint costs.

The News dominated its closest competitor, the Courier-Express, during the week. At the time of Blue Chip's acquisition, the News had circulation of 268,000 during the week. The Courier-Express had daily circulation of 123,000. However, the Courier-Express had circulation of 270,000 on Sunday due to the lack of competition.[47] If the News could capture enough market share on Sunday, then the business could produce abnormal profits as the dominant Buffalo paper.

After Blue Chip bought the News, the company began publishing a Sunday paper. However, this led to multiple years of difficulty for the News. In 1978, the Courier-Express was selling 100,000 more papers than the News on Sunday.[48] Additionally, legal troubles began to mount. The Courier-Express filed a lawsuit against the News after the company launched the Sunday paper. The Courier-Express argued that Blue Chip was attempting to create a monopoly newspaper in Buffalo. For a while, this argument succeeded in the courts, and restrictions were placed on the News. These problems led to the News reporting a pretax operating loss of $2.9 million in 1978.[49] Eventually, the courts ruled that the antitrust laws attempted to promote competition among businesses, and the News was allowed to

107

challenge the Courier-Express on Sundays. Over time, the News became the leader in terms of circulation on Sunday. By 1982, the Courier-Express went out of business and profits at the News began to pour in.

> "Six years ago, prior to introduction of a Sunday edition of the News, the long-established Courier-Express, as the only Sunday newspaper published in Buffalo, had circulation of 272,000. The News now has Sunday circulation of 367,000, a 35% gain – even though the number of households within the primary circulation area has shown little change during the six years."
> -Warren Buffett's 1982 Letter to Berkshire Hathaway Shareholders

The population of Erie County, where the News was located, was 1,015,000 in 1980.[50] The circulation of the News reached 367,000 by 1982,[51] or 36.2% of the entire population of Erie County. Considering that many families consisted of multiple people who shared one paper, the News reached an extremely large portion of the Buffalo population. This made advertising within the News more valuable for local businesses. The financials of the News eventually reflected this value. Sales reached $107.9 million in 1985, while net income amounted to $14 million.[52] Although the News had to go through some years of losses, the profits in 1985 alone made up 39.4% of the price Blue Chip paid to acquire the News. With such a dominant position in Buffalo, the News appeared destined for significant profitability for years to come.

Buffalo News	1978	1980	1983	1985
Sales	$44,791,000	$49,977,000	$90,161,000	$107,864,000
CAGR		5.6%	34.3%	9.4%
Net Income	-$738,000	-$816,000	$8,518,000	$13,980,000
CAGR				28.1%

Pinkerton's

In 1977, Blue Chip invested in a company called Pinkerton's.[53] The business began in 1850 as a detective agency,[54] mostly for railroad companies. Throughout the late 1800's, the firm also provided protection for industrial companies against striking labor unions. Pinkerton's developed a controversial reputation after some confrontations with labor unions turned violent. By the mid 1970's, the firm provided security guards and investigative services to businesses, hospitals, schools, and events. Although the company's history is controversial, the brand name was still unique due to the folklore from many fictional books, movies, and television shows portraying the detective agency over the years.

In the 10 years leading up to Blue Chip's investment in Pinkerton's, the business grew its sales and profits every single year. In 1966, sales were $71.4 million, while net income was $1.9 million.[55] In 1976, sales came in at $215.4 million, while net income was $8 million.[56] Sales and profits compounded over this period at 11.7% and 15.3% per year, respectively. This appeared to be a consistent business growing at a steady rate.

	1966	1976
Sales	$71,372,941	$215,420,000
CAGR		11.7%
Net Income	$1,936,272	$8,041,000
CAGR		15.3%

As you might expect for a service business, the company needed little capital to operate. This was reflected in the return on assets figure, which was in the double digits throughout the entire decade. The return on assets ranged from 14% to 17.4%. The return on equity ranged from 18.2% to 26%. This return on equity was achieved without the use of any debt. The company's liabilities were mostly in the form of accounts payable. Pinkerton's kept plenty of cash on hand as well. Excluding cash, the return on equity would have looked even better, ranging from 36.8% to 47.4%.

In 1972, the stock price of Pinkerton's reached $91.50 per share.[57] This gave the company a market value of $253.9 million.[58] During 1973, the stock price crashed all the way down to $16 per share.[59] After this 82.5% drop, the company was selling for just $44.4 million. Even though the stock price crashed, the business was doing just fine. Sales were up 8.1% in 1973, while net income increased 13.8%. The company also increased its dividend by 4%.

It is interesting to look at how quickly the valuation changed for Pinkerton's in the early 1970's. An investor in 1972 would have owned a company that earned $5.5 million in the prior year, while the company was valued at $253.9 million. This would give investors in Pinkerton's an initial yield of 2.1%. Since the 10 year treasury rate was 6.4% in 1972, this implies that the market expected the company to grow its profits in the future.[60] The following year the market value of Pinkerton's dropped to $44.4 million, giving investors an initial yield of 12.3%. The 10 year treasury rate increased slightly to 6.7% in 1973. Pinkerton's was consistently growing its profits, but the stock price implied low expectations for the future of the company in 1973. The valuation turned very pessimistic.

	1972	1973	1974
High Stock Price	$91.50	$69.75	$26.50
Low Stock Price	$49.50	$16.00	$16.25
Market Value High	$253,912,500	$193,556,250	$73,537,500
Market Value Low	$137,362,500	$44,400,000	$45,093,750

In the 1978 Annual Report, Blue Chip reported a $23.4 million investment in Pinkerton's. $19.2 million was invested in the Class A stock, while the remainder was invested in the Class B stock. Blue Chip's ownership of Pinkerton's came at an average cost of $32.69 per share, which valued Pinkerton's at $90.7 million.[61] This single investment made up 37.4% of Blue Chip's marketable securities portfolio in 1978 at cost. Blue Chip invested $23.4 million, while the entire portfolio was carried at $62.4 million.[62] This is an example of Buffett and Munger's willingness to bet heavily when an investment appears attractive enough. Pinkerton's had $23.3 million of cash on the balance sheet, so the company was selling for $67.4 million net of cash. The firm earned $8 million the year before, and paid out $4 million in dividends.[63] This valuation gave investors an initial yield of 11.9% based on profits, and a dividend yield of 6%. For comparison, the 10 year treasury rate was 7.4% in 1977. Although Blue Chip owned over 25% of Pinkerton's, the company was not accounted for as an equity method investment. Some of the stock Blue Chip owned did not have voting rights, so Blue Chip was not considered to have significant influence or control over Pinkerton's. Due to this, only the dividends paid by Pinkerton's showed up in Blue Chip's net income figure reported on the income statement. Although meaningful economically, the rest of its share of Pinkerton's profits were not accounted for within Blue Chip's financial statements.

In December 1982, a company named American Brands announced that they would acquire Pinkerton's for $77.50 per share.[64] This was 137.1% above Blue Chip's cost. The company earned a compound annual growth rate of 15% on the investment.[65] Berkshire had the opportunity to acquire Pinkerton's, presumably before American Brands made its offer. However, Berkshire decided to pass on the acquisition due to the potential legal liability associated with providing guards at airports and other locations. Berkshire was becoming a huge organization with an incredible amount of financial assets, which meant that it would have been a target for lawsuits if something were to have gone wrong with Pinkerton's guards.

Although it never happened, Pinkerton's would have sent plenty of cash to Buffett and Munger had Blue Chip acquired the entire company. Blue Chip invested $23.4 million into Pinkerton's at a time when the business was valued at $90.7 million. Blue Chip purchased over 25% of Pinkerton's, and by 1982 this ownership grew to 37% of the company. Pinkerton's had $23.3

111

million of cash on the balance sheet in 1976. Given the capital-light nature of the business, Blue Chip potentially could have taken $20 million out of the business right away since it really wasn't needed to run the operations of Pinkerton's. From 1978 to 1981, Pinkerton's reported net income of $53.8 million.[66] Within just four years, there is a good chance that Blue Chip could have earned back 81.3% of its purchase price in cash. All of this could have been achieved without even leveraging the business in terms of debt. Buffett and Munger could have used that cash to invest in more businesses that produced even more sources of cash flow.

1977 Excess Cash	$20,000,000
Cumulative Net Income 1978 - 1981	$53,786,000
Total Cash	**$73,786,000**
1977 Valuation	$90,714,750
Percent Yield	**81.3%**

Wesco Financial

Wesco Financial was the parent company that owned Mutual Savings and Loan of Pasadena, California. Blue Chip began buying the stock of Wesco in 1972.[67] During that year, Wesco had a market value of between $28.5 million and $41.2 million.[68] Wesco reported total equity of $59.7 million in the previous year, far greater than the price Wesco was selling for in the market.[69] At the low point of 1972, the valuation for Wesco was only 47.8% of its total reported equity value. Wesco earned profits of $3.1 million for the year, which was a yield of 11% based on the low price of 1972. The 10 year treasury rate was 6.4% in 1972.[70]

After Blue Chip purchased Wesco stock, Financial Corporation of Santa Barbara proposed a deal to merge with Wesco. Buffett and Munger thought that the terms of the merger were far too low for Wesco shareholders, so they decided to buy more Wesco stock in an attempt to take control of the company. By 1975, Blue Chip owned 64.4% of Wesco.[71] Blue Chip increased its ownership of Wesco to 80.1% by 1977.[72]

Participants in the savings and loan business (S&L) had an advantage over other banks in terms of attracting deposits. There were regulations surrounding the level of rates that firms could pay on deposits. Members of an S&L association were allowed to pay 0.5% higher on their deposits, which helped attract customers. Regulators at the time allowed this in order to encourage home ownership in the U.S. The thought was that higher deposits at an S&L would lead to growth in the amount of mortgages in the system, making it easier for citizens to buy a house. An S&L was required to have a majority of its assets involved in residential mortgages. Additionally, each S&L had to meet reserve requirements set by the Federal Savings and Loan Corporation.

While Wesco had some competitive advantages and was selling for a price that looked statistically cheap, there were issues with the S&L industry. Financial institutions, like banks, typically borrow money from depositors and then earn income by lending to borrowers. The S&L industry had the tendency to borrow short and lend long. Firms would borrow short by taking in short-term demand deposits from clients. These demand deposits had little to no restrictions, so clients could withdraw their money at any time. Firms would then lend long by making long term fixed rate mortgage loans. This type of business plan opened up the S&L industry to interest rate risk, as well as funding risks.

Wesco, and other financial institutions like it, made money on the spread between what it paid depositors and what it charged lenders. When the duration of deposits and loans do not come close to matching, a firm can run into trouble. When interest rates change, short-term deposits would be affected before the change is reflected within long-term mortgage loans. If interest rates rise, then depositors will be paid higher rates. If rates rise too much, then the yield earned on loans may be insufficient to cover the rate paid to depositors. When the duration of deposits and loans match, then the

113

rate earned on the asset side would offset the rate paid on the liability side and the firm would face less trouble regarding changes in interest rates.

A financial institution can also experience risks from its sources of funding. When the firm collects money from short-term depositors, there is a chance these clients could withdraw their money and leave. With loans extending out many years into the future, the firm could end up not having enough money on hand to fund its asset base. Liquidity issues like this can be a serious threat to financial institutions.

	1973	1977	1980
Loans Receivable	$389,584,000	$394,125,000	$164,648,000
Total Equity	$67,551,000	$81,409,000	$102,957,000
Loans/Equity	5.77	4.84	1.60

In 1973, Wesco had loans of $389.6 million against total equity of $67.6 million. Loans accounted for 86.2% of the firm's $452 million in assets. These loans were mostly funded with savings accounts, as the $67.6 million of total equity was just a fraction of the loans outstanding. Deposits amounted to 88.7% of Wesco's amount of loans on the balance sheet.[73] As the decade went on, Wesco reduced its overall leverage and became much more liquid. By 1977, loans represented 67.8% of Wesco's assets, while cash and bonds made up 17.9%.[74] Additionally, the common stock portfolio grew after Buffett and Munger took over. In 1973, common stocks represented just 1.5% of assets.[75] By 1977, common stocks at market value amounted to 10.1% of assets.[76] Wesco had additional liquidity to fall back on in the late 1970's.

	1973	1977	1980
Cash	$1,151,000	$1,614,000	$2,234,000
Bonds	$32,176,000	$102,348,000	$73,982,000
Stocks	$6,785,000	$58,136,000	$84,631,000
Loans	$389,584,000	$394,125,000	$164,648,000
Other Assets	$22,284,000	$24,871,000	$36,030,000
Total Assets	**$451,980,000**	**$581,094,000**	**$361,525,000**

	1973	1977	1980
Cash	0.3%	0.3%	0.6%
Bonds	7.1%	17.6%	20.5%
Stocks	1.5%	10.0%	23.4%
Loans	86.2%	67.8%	45.5%
Other Assets	4.9%	4.3%	10.0%
Total Assets	100.0%	100.0%	100.0%

"Results were good for shareholders before 1981-82 only because interest rates were stable or rose slowly as mortgage-loan portfolios steadily and rapidly expanded under a regulatory structure which both fostered growth and protected operating margins by requiring that on all insured savings accounts fixed rates be paid that were slightly higher than the low rates specified for banks. Thus a small deposit-attracting rate advantage over banks was given to savings and loan associations, while competitive pressure was dampened for both types of institutions."
-Charlie Munger's 1983 Letter to Wesco Shareholders

While the industry was lucky for a while due to cooperative interest rates as well as the regulatory environment, this would not last forever. As the risks surrounding the S&L industry continued to intensify, Wesco decided to divest most of its assets in that business. In December 1980, Wesco sold all of its branches except the home office. $307 million of deposits were sold, as

115

well as an equal amount of mortgages. Wesco received $8.1 million on the sale.[77]

Following the divestiture, the amount of loans on the balance sheet dropped from $506.2 million in 1979 to $164.6 million in 1980. The total equity of Wesco amounted to $103 million, which was 62.5% of loans outstanding. The company held on to $168.4 million of deposits as well. In terms of assets, cash and bonds made up 21.1% of Wesco's total assets in 1980, while common stocks represented another 23.4%. Loans amounted to 45.5% of assets that year.[78] The S&L business of Wesco was clearly scaled back in 1980, which led to the company having plenty of excess capital.

Throughout the 1980's, Wesco continued to shift away from its traditional business. The company developed a significant investment in equity securities, with the portfolio reaching $111.5 million in 1983.[79] This portfolio earned extraordinary returns. In 1984 and 1985, Wesco reported a pretax gain on the sale of securities of $19.4 million and $62.9 million, respectively.[80] The company's entire net income in 1983 was just $10.6 million.[81] Most of the huge gain in 1985 can be attributed to an investment in General Foods Corporation, which was acquired by Philip Morris that year. Wesco recognized a $34.4 million after-tax gain on sale from its investment in General Foods alone.[82] This was a significant source of shareholder value, as Wesco had total equity of $124.1 million in 1983,[83] and $163.6 million in 1984. Following the gain from the General Foods investment, total equity for Wesco reached $190.8 million at the end of 1985.[84]

Wesco further expanded its business into insurance in 1985. The company internally formed Wesco-Financial Insurance Company (Wes-FIC) as a co-venture with Berkshire Hathaway. Wes-FIC was formed to do business in the reinsurance industry specifically. Wesco had an abundance of excess capital at the time, so the reinsurance business made sense. Companies that did business with Wes-FIC could trust the promises made by Wesco and Berkshire related to insurance agreements. Wesco and Berkshire were reliable due to their abundant capital, low leverage, diversified earning power, and history of retaining earnings.

> "With the enthusiastic approval of all Wesco's directors, including substantial Wesco shareholders in the Peters and Caspers families, without whose approval such action would not have been taken, Wesco invested $45,000,000 in cash equivalents in a newly organized, wholly owned, Nebraska-chartered insurance company, Wesco-Financial Insurance Company ("Wes-FIC")."
>
> -Charlie Munger's 1985 Letter to Wesco Shareholders

At Wesco, Buffett and Munger continued to follow a similar playbook as they did with Berkshire and Blue Chip. They used excess capital to invest in new businesses. Then, they used the profits from those businesses to buy more businesses. Wesco became another compounding machine.

General Foods Corporation

General Foods Corporation was a company that owned many popular food and beverage brands in the U.S. Its largest segment in the 1980's was Packaged Grocery Products, led by brands such as Post cereals, Jell-O, and Cool Whip.[85] Coffee was another important segment for the company, which was sold in grocery stores under the Maxwell House brand. Other beverage products manufactured by General Foods included Kool-Aid, Country Time, and Tang.

Both Wesco and Berkshire disclosed an investment in General Foods in 1979, but the companies invested much more heavily in 1980 and 1983. Combining Berkshire's ownership through Wesco, Berkshire invested $62.5 million at a price of $31.51 per share as of the end of 1980.[86] By the end of 1983, Berkshire had paid a total of $163.8 million for its General Foods stock at a price of $36.79 per share.[87] This was a sizable investment for the company, as Berkshire had total equity of $1.1 billion in 1983.[88]

General Foods had been growing at a solid rate through the 1970's. Revenue compounded at a rate of 11% from 1971[89] to 1979, while net income grew 8.7% compounded annually over the period.[90] The firm enjoyed double digit returns on equity during this time period as well. General Foods produced a return on equity of 17.6% in 1979. The company earned $232.1 million that year, which gave Berkshire an initial yield of 14.8% based on the $1.6 billion valuation it paid for its stock.

	1971	1979
Revenue	$2,390,000,000	$5,508,079,000
CAGR		11.0%
Net Income	$119,000,000	$232,149,000
CAGR		8.7%

The growth continued for General Foods in the early part of the 1980's. Sales grew to $9.1 billion in 1985, which was a compound annual growth rate of 8.7% since 1979. Net income increased as well, with the company reporting profits of $324.9 million that year.[91] As profits increased, the stock price followed suit. At the end of 1984, Berkshire's General Foods investment was showing a gain of 50.9%.[92]

"When Wesco made its investment in General Foods stock several years ago, because General Foods' executives seemed sensible and the stock was available in the market at a conservative price relative to its value as a share of ownership in a presumably ever-continuing independent entity, it was unprecedented and virtually inconceivable that a corporation the size of General Foods would ever be "bear-hugged" into selling out at an immense premium over the then prevailing market price for its stock. But that is what happened, wholly unpredicted by Wesco, in 1985 as old taboos eroded and the great American takeover game swept into new areas."
-Charlie Munger's 1985 Letter to Wesco Shareholders

Leveraged buyouts were all the rage at the time, and General Foods ended up being a takeover candidate. Philip Morris paid $120 per share to acquire the company near the end of 1985.[93] Berkshire finished accumulating shares of General Foods in 1983, and just two years later the company was bought out at more than triple the price. The price Philip Morris paid was steep, as it valued the company at $5.9 billion. The price Berkshire paid gave the company an initial yield of 14.8%, but Philip Morris' price yielded 5.5% based on 1985 earnings. Berkshire's investment went up in value partially because of increased earnings at General Foods, but mostly because the market was willing to pay a higher valuation for the company in 1985 than it was in the early 1980's.

Berkshire reported a $227.8 million after-tax gain on the sale of General Foods stock in 1985,[94] including Wesco's gain on sale of $34.4 million.[95] Wesco had total equity of $163.6 million the year before, so this gain alone was 21% of beginning equity.[96] The after-tax gain on sale for Berkshire amounted to a return of 17.9% based on its equity in 1984.[97] The work Buffett and Munger went through to make this investment took five years, while the income only hit the income statement in 1985. This means that reported net income overstated normalized earning power that year, but also that earnings were understated in the years leading up to 1985. Eventually, General Foods merged with Kraft Foods. Kraft Foods merged with Heinz in 2015, which led to Berkshire becoming an investor in the company again.

Detroit International Bridge Company

The Detroit International Bridge Company owned and operated a toll bridge that connected Detroit, Michigan with Windsor, Ontario. Named the Ambassador Bridge, it opened for traffic in November 1929.[98] The bridge stretches over the Detroit River, and provides a route for a large amount of commercial traffic between the U.S. and Canada. Berkshire Hathaway owned stock in the bridge going back to at least 1972, and Wesco owned a large chunk of the business in the late 1970's.

> "I have said in an inflationary world that a toll bridge would be a great thing to own if it was unregulated...Because you have laid out the capital costs. You build the bridge in old dollars and you don't have to keep replacing it."
> -Warren Buffett, *Courier-Express v. Evening News* testimony[99]

A toll bridge isn't a very complicated business to understand. Although there would be capital expenditures in terms of maintenance each year, the bridge would only need to be built once. As inflation occurs over time, the owner of the bridge can hopefully adjust toll rates accordingly. A bridge owner would especially have pricing power if motorists have limited travel options. While the Detroit & Canada Tunnel was a competitor right down the river, about 85% of the trucking traffic chose the Ambassador Bridge.[100] Overall traffic numbers were similar between the two, but the Ambassador Bridge dominated the commercial traffic.

Although the Detroit International Bridge Company owned tangible assets and produced consistent levels of cash flow, the company was debt free. This could be partially attributed to the fact that the company went bankrupt in the late 1930's, not too long after the bridge was constructed. After emerging from bankruptcy, the company had a very conservative balance sheet. In 1976, 54.8% of the company's assets were made up of cash.[101] The remaining assets were mostly property related to the bridge. The company's liabilities were minimal, as equity made up 86.8% of total assets. The company had some firepower stored up in case management wanted to become more aggressive, especially if it became a part of a diversified holding company.

The Detroit International Bridge Company was a great business. From 1968 to 1977, the return on assets was over 20% every single year. Since the company had little in terms of liabilities, the return on equity was pretty similar. However, the company had quite a bit of excess cash. If you removed cash, the company's return on equity would have ranged from 37.7% to 74.8% over the period. Sales compounded at an annual growth rate of 8.7%.

The company only experienced a decrease in sales in two of those years.[102] This was a reliable business.

	1968	1971	1974	1977
Sales	$3,996,264	$5,014,724	$7,347,991	$8,440,000
CAGR		7.9%	13.6%	4.7%
Net Income	$1,240,553	$1,475,128	$2,437,437	$2,320,000
CAGR		5.9%	18.2%	-1.6%
Equity	$4,697,193	$6,073,255	$8,452,494	$9,295,000
Return on Equity (ROE)	26.4%	24.3%	28.8%	25.0%
Cash	$1,917,022	$2,381,084	$4,958,451	$5,127,000
ROE Excluding Cash	44.6%	40.0%	69.8%	55.7%

Although sales increased throughout the 1970's, toll rates remained unchanged since 1971.[103] The increase in sales was only due to higher traffic on the bridge. Since the Ambassador Bridge was the clear favorite among commercial traffic, you would think that the bridge would have the opportunity to raise rates eventually. A new entrant would have to spend millions, as well as sort through regulatory issues, in order to build a new bridge. As long as the toll rate increases didn't get out of hand, it would be reasonable to see rates improve over time. With consistent operating profitability, excess liquidity, the opportunity to increase leverage, and potentially untapped pricing power, the Detroit International Bridge Company looked like an attractive investment opportunity.

In 1977, the company sold for between $19 million and $29.5 million.[104] At the same time, cash amounted to $5.6 million on the balance sheet. This means that the business sold for between $13.4 million and $23.9 million net of cash. The bridge produced profits of $2.4 million in the previous year, and paid out $1.7 million in dividends to shareholders. This would mean an initial earnings yield of between 10.2% and 18.1% at 1977 stock prices.[105] Since the

121

10 year treasury rate was 7.7% in 1977, this looked like a cheap price to pay for such a high quality asset.[106]

Berkshire had been buying stock in the Detroit International Bridge Company throughout the early 1970's. By 1974, Berkshire's average cost on the stock was $13.34 adjusting for stock dividends. The total cost for Berkshire was $560,430.[107] This was a small investment for Berkshire, as it only represented 1.1% of the common stock portfolio. In 1977, Wesco invested more heavily in the stock. By November 1977, Wesco owned 21.6% of the company[108] at a cost of $20 per share.[109] This valued Detroit International Bridge Company at about $25.4 million. Wesco invested $5.5 million into the company, which was 8.6% of its total marketable securities portfolio at the time.[110] Wesco attempted to acquire all of the Detroit International Bridge Company, but was outbid. Central Cartage Company, owned by Manuel Moroun, ended up buying out the bridge for $24 per share. Central Cartage paid 20% above Wesco's average cost. Once the bridge was taken private, this resulted in a realized profit of $1 million for Wesco.[110]

Precision Steel Warehouse

In February 1979, Wesco acquired Precision Steel Warehouse. Precision was located in Franklin Park, Illinois. Wesco paid $15.1 million for the business.[111] Precision was a private business, so we are unable to fully analyze the company's financials prior to the acquisition. From what was disclosed following the acquisition, we can see that Precision earned $1.9 million in 1978 before becoming a part of Wesco.[112] This was a yield of 12.7% for the year based on the purchase price. In 1979, the annual report provided a breakdown of Precision's assets and liabilities as a part of Wesco. The reported profits for 1978 would have amounted to a return on assets of 11.4%.[113] Precision had minimal liabilities, so the return on equity was a similar value, coming in at 13.2% in 1979.[114]

Precision Steel	
Net Income - 1978	$1.9 million
Return on Assets	11.4%
Return on Equity	13.2%

The capital of Precision Steel basically consisted of property, plant, and equipment, receivables, and inventory. Total liabilities amounted to 14.3% of assets, while equity made up the other 85.7%.[115] There were little working capital benefits in terms of accounts payable or other liabilities, so the vast majority of the capital of the business was funded with equity. This situation could shine some light on the competitive position of the business. Precision Steel took on some of the capital from customers in terms of accounts receivable, while the company had less in accounts payable from its suppliers. However, Precision Steel was able to earn an acceptable return on this capital. The return on both assets and equity was consistently in the double digits.

Precision Steel - 1979		
Cash	$1,413,000	8.4%
Accounts Receivable	$4,659,000	27.6%
Inventory	$6,082,000	36.0%
PPE	$4,410,000	26.1%
Other steel assets	$329,000	1.9%
Total Steel Assets	**$16,893,000**	**100.0%**
Notes Payable	$307,000	1.8%
Accounts Payable	$1,870,000	11.1%
Income Tax Liability	$236,000	1.4%
Total Steel Liabilities	**$2,413,000**	**14.3%**
Total Steel Equity	**$14,480,000**	**85.7%**

The Precision Steel acquisition cost Wesco $15.1 million, or 15.7% of the $95.9 million in total equity Wesco had at the end of 1979. Wesco earned $11.1 million that year, with Precision Steel accounting for $1.7 million after-tax, or 15.3%.[116] While the results might not have been spectacular, Precision Steel diversified the earning power of Blue Chip, and produced cash for Wesco to reinvest. Precision Steel was able to produce a few million dollars in profits in most years through 1985, which was attractive based on what Wesco paid for the business. Precision Steel earned an initial yield of 12.7% for Wesco based on the purchase price, and this yield grew slightly over time. From 1979 to 1985, revenue for Precision Steel compounded at a rate of 5.2% per year, while net income compounded at a rate of 2.8%. Precision Steel earned $2 million in 1985, or 13.3% of the original purchase price.[117]

124

Precision Steel	1979	1985
Revenue	$37,883,000	$51,305,000
CAGR		5.2%
Net Income	$1,707,000	$2,010,000
CAGR		2.8%

Blue Chip Stamps

Blue Chip first appeared in the Berkshire annual report in 1972 as an investment within the equity portfolio of the insurance company. In the few years leading up to this, limited disclosure was given regarding which stocks were held in the portfolio. In 1972, Berkshire owned 853,754 shares of Blue Chip at a cost of $13.22 per share. Berkshire's total cost amounted to $11.3 million. However, the stock price had increased 16.3%, leading to a market value of $13.1 million that year. Blue Chip represented 41.3% of the entire portfolio of marketable securities in 1972. Cleveland Cliffs Iron Company accounted for 12% of the portfolio, while California Water Service Company, Kennecott Copper Corporation, and National Presto Industries rounded out the top 5 positions. The top 5 positions accounted for 71.7% of the portfolio, while the rest was made up of small positions in 28 other stocks.[118]

1972	Market Value	% of Portfolio
Blue Chip Stamps	$13,130,968	41.3%
Cleveland Cliffs Iron Company	$3,829,962	12.0%
California Water Service Company	$2,406,211	7.6%
Kennecott Copper Corporation	$1,790,750	5.6%
National Presto Industries	$1,671,413	5.3%
Other	$8,999,828	28.3%
Total Marketable Securities	**$31,829,132**	100.0%

The 853,754 shares of stock owned by Berkshire in 1972 represented ownership of 16.9% of Blue Chip.[119] However, Buffett owned additional stock through Diversified Retailing. Buffett, and therefore Berkshire, had a controlling interest in Blue Chip. Due to this, the Blue Chip investment was accounted for as an equity method investment within Berkshire's balance sheet. This means that Berkshire's 16.9% share of Blue Chip's earnings would be presented within the income statement of Berkshire as well. Berkshire received dividends of $111,168 from Blue Chip, but no additional income was recognized in 1972 as the earnings were insignificant after accounting for the expense related to amortization of goodwill.[120]

Berkshire increased its ownership of Blue Chip throughout the 1970's. At first, this increase in ownership was a direct result of purchasing stock in the open market. Later, the merger of the Diversified Retailing into Berkshire was responsible for increasing Berkshire's ownership from 36.5%[121] to 58%.[122] In 1983, Blue Chip was also merged into Berkshire, resulting in Berkshire's full ownership of the Blue Chip.

Berkshire's Ownership of Blue Chip Stamps	Shares	Ownership
1972	853,754	16.9%
1973	989,483	19.1%
1974	1,325,233	25.6%
1975	1,325,233	25.6%
1976	1,720,709	33.2%
1977	1,890,335	36.5%
1978	3,003,820	58.0%
1979	3,107,400	60.0%
1980	3,107,400	60.0%
1981	3,107,400	60.0%
1982	3,107,400	60.0%
1983	-	100.0%

Blue Chip had total assets of $147.3 million at the end of February 1970, and 76.2% of that was made up of stocks and bonds. Inventory was the next largest asset at 12.9%, followed by 2.4% for prepaid expenses. Property, plant, and equipment represented just 2% of assets. The liability from unredeemed trading stamps was the largest line item on the liability side, representing 58.5% of total assets. Blue Chip had payables of 10.1% of assets, followed by debt amounting to 7.4% of assets. The company's total equity was 24% of assets at the time.[123] This was an extremely capital-light business.

Blue Chip	February 1970	% of Assets
Cash	$468,000	0.3%
Marketable Securities	$112,288,000	76.2%
Accounts Receivable	$6,704,000	4.6%
Inventories	$19,011,000	12.9%
Prepaid Expenses	$3,504,000	2.4%
Property, Plant, and Equipment	$2,928,000	2.0%
Unamortized Debt Discount	$2,430,000	1.6%
Total Assets	**$147,333,000**	**100.0%**
Accounts Payable	$7,851,000	5.3%
Income Taxes Payable	$7,022,000	4.8%
Liability for Unredeemed Trading Stamps	$86,189,000	58.5%
Notes Payable to Banks	$10,840,000	7.4%
Total liabilities	**$111,902,000**	**76.0%**
Stockholders Equity	$35,431,000	24.0%
Total Liabilities and Equity	**$147,333,000**	**100.0%**

In 1970, Blue Chip reported $14.8 million of earnings before interest and taxes (EBIT). A meaningful portion of this EBIT came from interest income and dividends earned on the marketable securities portfolio. Net income for the year amounted to $8.6 million, which was a 19.8% return on equity. Blue Chip paid shareholders a $1.2 million dividend, but retained the remainder of the profits.[124] The following year, stamp service revenue dropped by 15%. This led to a lower operating profit figure of $5.9 million for the year. The company also realized losses of $1.7 million on marketable securities for the year, leading to net income of $4.2 million.[125] Blue Chip again paid out $1.2 million in dividends and retained the rest of the profits.[126]

In January 1972, Blue Chip purchased See's Candy for $35 million, or $25.1 million net of cash acquired. Blue Chip took on $32.7 million of

128

additional debt to fund the acquisition.[127] Even after taking into account the money spent on this acquisition, Blue Chip still finished the year with $25 million more in marketable securities than when the year began. See's had excess cash on hand when it was acquired, and Blue Chip also saw increased cash flow from changes in working capital that year in terms of an increase in float.

For the rest of the 1970's, See's fueled the growth of Blue Chip. Stamp service revenue declined from $88.7 million[128] in 1972 to $18.3 million in 1979.[129] See's had sales of $32 million in 1972, its first year within Blue Chip. Candy sales reached $87.3 million by 1979. Following the decrease in its traditional stamp business, the float at Blue Chip declined as well. However, the decline in float was not as dramatic as the decline in sales. The liability for unredeemed trading stamps went from $93.4 million in 1972 to $67.5 million in 1979. Some customers who received trading stamps never exchanged the stamps for free products. Others redeemed stamps slowly over time. See's alone earned a pretax operating profit of $12.8 million in 1979, while all of Blue Chip only earned $11.9 million pretax in 1972.[130]

	1972	1979
Stamp Service Revenue	$88,736,000	$18,277,000
Growth		-79.4%
Candy Sales	$32,049,000	$87,314,000
Growth		172.4%
Liability for Unredeemed Trading Stamps	$93,351,000	$67,524,000
Growth		-27.7%

By March 1973, Blue Chip owned a portfolio of stocks that cost $123.3 million. Blue Chip owned 21.9% of Wesco Financial at the time. The Wesco stake cost $8.1 million, so it represented 6.6% of the total portfolio. By April 1974, Blue Chip's ownership in Wesco increased to 57%.[131] Eventually, Blue

Chip acquired 80% of Wesco and it was no longer listed in the marketable securities portfolio since it was a controlled business. Additionally, Blue Chip spent $34 million to buy the Buffalo Evening News in 1977.[132] Both of these items led to a decrease in the dollar value allocated to the marketable securities portfolio on Blue Chip's balance sheet. Blue Chip sold a portion of their marketable securities portfolio and took out an additional $11.4 million in debt to fund the Buffalo News acquisition.

12/30/1978	% of Portfolio*	Cost	Market Value	% Gain
Bonds	18.6%	$14,238,000	$14,238,000	0.0%
American Waterworks	1.2%	$1,062,000	$955,000	-10.1%
Cleveland-Cliffs Iron Company	16.8%	$13,222,000	$12,845,000	-2.9%
CloveTrust Corporation	1.8%	$1,211,000	$1,362,000	12.5%
Manufacturers National Corporation	5.4%	$3,706,000	$4,146,000	11.9%
National Detroit Corporation	15.4%	$9,941,000	$11,752,000	18.2%
Pinkerton's, Inc.	21.3%	$19,201,000	$16,300,000	-15.1%
Pittsburgh National Corporation	12.1%	$8,721,000	$9,234,000	5.9%
San Jose Water Works	2.1%	$1,462,000	$1,638,000	12.0%
Other	5.3%	$3,869,000	$4,024,000	4.0%
Total Marketable Equity Securities	81.4%	$62,395,000	$62,256,000	-0.2%
Total Portfolio	**100.0%**	**$76,633,000**	**$76,494,000**	**-0.2%**

*At Market Value

At the end of 1972, Berkshire owned 16.9% of Blue Chip. This investment cost Berkshire $11.3 million, and valued Blue Chip at $66.6 million. Blue Chip earned $7.1 million, or 10.7% of Berkshire's cost basis. However, included in this net income was an expense related to a legal settlement of $925,000 as well as $82,000 in realized losses on investment securities. Excluding these expenses, Blue Chip earned an after-tax operating profit of $8.1 million. This would give Berkshire a yield of 12.2% based on its cost basis. Blue Chip had total equity of $53.1 million that year, which means that Berkshire's position cost 25.4% above the 1972 book value.[133]

During the market decline of the mid 1970's, the valuation of Blue Chip became completely absurd. The stock price of Blue Chip reached a high of $19.75 per share in 1971, but fell 77.2% to $4.50 per share in 1974.[134] Berkshire's investment fell to 66% below its 1972 cost basis. At the low point, Blue Chip was selling for a valuation of $23.3 million. This was an incredible bargain. Just a few years earlier, Blue Chip paid $25.1 million for See's Candy alone. Blue Chip had total equity of $59.9 million, so the stock was selling for only 38.9% of its book value. This equity was made up of some valuable assets. Blue Chip owned $132.7 million worth of marketable securities, which made up two-thirds of the company's total assets.[135] The marketable securities portfolio contained $101.6 million of preferred and common stocks, while bonds made up another $31.2 million.[136] The company had $3 million of cash, along with millions of dollars in receivables, property, equipment, and inventory. These assets were funded by $78.8 million of float from trading stamps, as well as debt of $50.6 million.[137] The equity of Blue Chip contained liquid assets that could be sold for cash in the market. This was not a company that had worthless inventory or depreciated equipment sitting on the books. Additionally, two of the greatest investors in the history of the world controlled the marketable securities portfolio. By the 1970's, both Buffett and Munger had legendary track records.

	1973
Cash	$3,013,000
Bonds	$31,164,000
Stocks	$101,579,000
Other Assets	$64,464,000
Total Assets	**$200,220,000**
Liability for Unredeemed Trading Stamps	$78,776,000
Debt	$50,553,000
Other Liabilities	$11,004,000
Total Liabilities	**$140,333,000**
Total Equity	**$59,887,000**
Market Value - 1974 Low	**$23,305,500**
Price to Book Value	**38.9%**

While Blue Chip looked cheap when analyzing the balance sheet, the income statement looked equally appealing. Blue Chip earned net income of $8 million the prior year, or 34.3% of its market value.[138] This 34.3% yield could be earned while interest rates were only 7.4%.[139] If the business never grew, owners of the business would earn their investment back in less than three years. Blue Chip averaged net income of $7.1 million over the previous five years, so the profits in 1973 constituted close to normalized earning power and was not just one abnormally good year. While the traditional trading stamp business was declining, candy sales were on the rise. See's Candy increased its revenue in 1973 by 11.6%.[140] See's had a history of solid growth, and had the ability to increase prices at its stores. While no growth was needed to justify the stock price of Blue Chip, there was a reasonable possibility that Blue Chip would be able to grow over time.

Blue Chip earned a solid 13.4% return on equity in 1973.[141] However, this return on equity was achieved while most of its assets were in marketable securities. Only dividends, interest, and realized gains on the sale of securities were recognized in net income. Some of Blue Chip's stocks would grow in value over time though. The unrealized gains on securities were not recognized on the income statement annually, but would provide for the occasional boost to net income when eventually sold. Blue Chip had unrealized losses within its marketable securities portfolio in 1973, but it would be reasonable to assume some growth in value over the years with Buffett and Munger in charge.

During this time period, the company's stock was thinly traded. Part of the reason for the lack of trading volume could have been due to the fact that Berkshire and other related parties, such as Diversified Retailing, owned so much of the stock. Due to the lack of trading activity, the National Association of Insurance Commissioners (NAIC) Valuation Committee assigned a value for the Blue Chip stock that was held within Berkshire's insurance companies. Blue Chip was assigned a value of $7.25 per share in 1973, down 52.9% from $15.38 per share the year before.[142] At $7.25 per share, Blue Chip was valued at $37.5 million.[143] As the market declined some more in 1974, Blue Chip ended up being valued at $5.25 per share by the NAIC that year for a market value of $27.2 million.[144] However, Berkshire stated in its annual report that it disagreed with the valuation of its Blue Chip stock.

"The company does not believe that the statutory valuation is indicative of the fair market value of the substantial block of Blue Chip shares represented by the Berkshire Hathaway holdings of which these are a part."
-1974 Berkshire Hathaway Annual Report

While Blue Chip had many things going right, not everything was perfect. The company had been plagued with lawsuits. Blue Chip settled 11 lawsuits in 1972 alone for a grand total of $1.9 million.[145] The trading stamp industry went through much litigation during this time period regarding antitrust concerns, both from competing stamp companies and from supermarket merchants. Sales of the traditional stamp business declined heavily in 1973, down 42.1% from \$88.7 million in 1972 to \$51.4 million in 1973.[146] One reason for the decline in stamp sales was the rise of the discount supermarket. The habits of shoppers changed along with the changes taking place in the retail industry.

> "Trading stamps generally - and Blue Chip stamps are no exception - have taken a "licking" due to the advent of a new type of supermarket promotion loosely described as "discounting". When a grocery company "goes discount", it typically reduces the variety of sizes and brands, shortens operating hours and stops issuing trading stamps. It then uses the promotion dollars to advertise its discount policy."
> -Blue Chip Stamps 1974 Annual Report

While Berkshire had owned the stock of Blue Chip beforehand, it took advantage of the bargain prices in the 1970's to increase its ownership. Berkshire owned 16.9% of Blue Chip in 1972, and steadily increased its position throughout the decade. In 1975, Berkshire owned 25.6% of Blue Chip, and by 1979 its stake was up to 60% of the business. Blue Chip ended up merging into Berkshire in 1983.

Throughout the rest of the 1970's, Blue Chip continued expanding and compounding. The company earned \$20.4 million in 1980, almost as much as the entire company was selling for just six years earlier.[147] The company acquired the Buffalo Evening News as well as Precision Steel. However, most of the growth in profits came from See's Candy. In 1980, 47.1% of the pretax operating profit came from See's Candy.[148]

Pretax Operating Profit	1978	1979	1980
Candy	$12,482,000	$12,785,000	$15,031,000
Newspaper	-$2,913,000	-$4,617,000	-$2,805,000
Steel Service Center	-	$3,051,000	$2,972,000
Promotional Services	$2,151,000	$2,397,000	$7,699,000
Wesco Financial Activities	$1,861,000	$2,795,000	$3,404,000
Equity in Net Income of Mutual Savings	$6,482,000	$6,795,000	$5,625,000
Total Pretax Operating Profit	**$20,063,000**	**$23,206,000**	**$31,926,000**

Pretax Operating Profit	1978	1979	1980
Candy	62.2%	55.1%	47.1%
Newspaper	-14.5%	-19.9%	-8.8%
Steel Service Center	0.0%	13.1%	9.3%
Promotional Services	10.7%	10.3%	24.1%
Wesco Financial Activities	9.3%	12.0%	10.7%
Equity in Net Income of Mutual Savings	32.3%	29.3%	17.6%
Total Pretax Operating Profit	**100.0%**	**100.0%**	**100.0%**

The stock price of Blue Chip enjoyed a nice growth rate in the late 1970's. From the low point in 1974 until the high point in 1980, the stock price of Blue Chip compounded at a rate of 33.1%.[149] Part of this can be attributed to the fact that Blue Chip stock traded at too low of a value in 1974, but the company also achieved good operating performance. However, Blue Chip was still undervalued in 1980. It appears that the market did not

135

appreciate or understand the value being created within Blue Chip. The stock of Blue Chip traded between $16.50 and $25.00 per share in 1980. This valued the company between $85.5 million and $129.5 million. Blue Chip earned profits of $20.4 million in 1980. Investors could have purchased Blue Chip at an initial earnings yield of 15.7% to 23.9%. While this initial earnings yield suggests a cheap valuation, this is dampened a little bit by the fact that the 10 year treasury rate was 12.8% at the time.[151] When interest rates are higher, you would generally expect valuations of businesses to be lower. This would lead to higher initial earnings yields. However, Blue Chip had total equity of $145.5 million, which was greater than Blue Chip's valuation in 1980 even at the high point. The equity of Blue Chip was made up of some liquid assets. 56.1% of Blue Chip's asset base consisted of publicly traded marketable securities. Stocks were on the balance sheet for $134.2 million, while Wesco stock was carried at $29 million as an unconsolidated subsidiary. The Class B shares of Pinkerton's were carried at $4.2 million and listed separately on the balance sheet since they were illiquid. Additionally, Blue Chip had cash and short-term bonds of $20.1 million, or 6.7% of assets. Combined, this cash and publicly traded securities amounted to $202.1 million.[152] Buffett and Munger still had plenty of liquidity to work with inside of Blue Chip's portfolio.

In 1983, Blue Chip finally merged with Berkshire. The two companies had been intertwined for the better part of two decades. One reason the merger took so long could have been due to Blue Chip's undervaluation in the market. When the companies merged, Blue Chip had 5,179,000 shares of stock outstanding. Berkshire owned 60% of Blue Chip, so that left 2,071,600 shares of stock owned by other shareholders. Each share of Blue Chip stock was exchanged for 0.077 of a share of Berkshire stock.[153] This equated to 160,400 shares of Berkshire, and the shares outstanding at Berkshire increased by this amount in 1983. In 1984, the stock price of Berkshire traded for between $1,220 and $1,360 per share.[154] This meant that the merger gave Blue Chip a valuation of between $486.5 million and $542.3 million in 1984.

IX. The Conglomerate

Berkshire Hathaway

For the first handful of years following the National Indemnity acquisition, Berkshire accounted for the insurance business as an unconsolidated subsidiary. Typically, subsidiaries are unconsolidated when the parent company has significant influence over the business, but only owns between 20% to 50% of it. Berkshire owned all of National Indemnity in this case, which would usually result in National Indemnity being fully consolidated within Berkshire's financial statements. Since insurance was such a different type of business than Berkshire's traditional textile operations, Berkshire chose not to consolidate the financials. Investors at the time could still view the full financial statements of National Indemnity within Berkshire's 10-K though.

"The accompanying financial statements consolidate the accounts of Berkshire Hathaway Inc. with its wholly-owned noninsurance Canadian subsidiary. The accounts of National Indemnity Company, over 99% owned by Berkshire Hathaway Inc., and National Fire & Marine Insurance Company, 100% owned, are not consolidated. The statement of earnings reflects equity of Berkshire Hathaway Inc. in earnings, excluding unrealized investment gains, of these functionally independent operations, and the balance sheet valuation is at cost plus equity in such earnings since purchase in March 1967."
-1968 Berkshire Hathaway Annual Report

Berkshire began consolidating the results of the insurance business within the company's financial statements in 1973. By this time, it was clear that Berkshire's most important segment was insurance by a wide margin. The assets of the insurance business were more than 10 times higher than the textile assets owned by Berkshire in 1972. The insurance business was growing extremely fast, while textiles were declining over the same period.

Assets	1970	1971	1972
Insurance	$74,245,955	$123,313,932	$139,484,449
Change		$49,067,977	$16,170,517
Textiles	$15,082,246	$13,449,994	$12,940,104
Change		-$1,632,252	-$509,890

The asset growth within the insurance segment was driven by an increase in capital invested in the business, premium growth, and the retention of earnings accumulated over the period. The balance sheet of the insurance group shows the change in capital invested in the business over this time frame. Berkshire, as the parent company, invested $13 million of additional capital into the insurance business from 1970 to 1972. This is shown within the common stock and paid-in surplus lines on the balance sheet of the Berkshire Hathaway Insurance Group. Berkshire took on $3.8 million of additional debt to fund this expansion, as well as reinvested the earnings produced from other businesses like Illinois National. The change in unassigned surplus can mostly be attributed to retained earnings over the period. Unassigned surplus increased by $19.2 million from 1970[1] to 1972, while Berkshire reported and retained $15.8 million of net income over the period.[2]

Change in Equity of the Insurance Group	1970	1971	1972	Total
Change in Common Stock $10 Par Value	$500,000	$500,000	$0	**$1,000,000**
Change in Common Stock $100 Par Value	$0	$2,000,000	$500,000	**$2,500,000**
Change in Paid-in Surplus	$1,500,000	$6,000,000	$2,000,000	**$9,500,000**
Change in Unassigned Surplus	$1,763,621	$9,641,805	$7,838,155	**$19,243,581**
Total Change	**$3,763,621**	**$18,141,805**	**$10,338,155**	**$32,243,581**

From 1969 to 1972, the insurance segment experienced asset growth of $89.1 million. The equity of the insurance group increased by $32.2 million from retained earnings and from incremental investment from Berkshire. The rest of the asset growth was fueled by an increase in premium volume. Premiums earned within the insurance group rose from $25.3 million[3] in 1969 to $59.6 million in 1972.[4] As more revenue was generated, liabilities increased on the balance sheet for unearned premiums and loss adjustment expenses. These two line items increased by $36.9 million over the period, financing the remainder of the asset growth that the insurance group experienced.

Revenue	1970	1971	1972
Premiums Earned	$39,172,512	$60,867,206	$59,627,050
Growth		55.4%	-2.0%

140

Liabilities	1970	1971	1972
Unearned Premiums	$17,482,957	$25,516,268	$23,839,397
Growth		45.9%	-6.6%
Losses and Loss Adjustment Expense	$29,758,739	$52,990,625	$60,275,018
Growth		78.1%	13.7%

As Berkshire expanded further into the insurance field, money came pouring in. The company earned $12.1 million in 1972, but cash flow from operations was $20.6 million.[5] The reason why cash flow was so much better than accounting profits was due to the float generated by the insurance business. Buffett was able to invest this cash in marketable securities.

The increase in premium volume turned out to be profitable, as the company experienced multiple years of underwriting profits. Premiums earned increased by 55.4% in 1971,[6] and remained at a similar level for the following two years.[7] The insurance group reported an underwriting profit of $9 million in total from 1971 to 1973. Additionally, Berkshire earned solid levels of investment income from the float.

	1970	1971	1972	1973
Underwriting Gain	-$1,981,481	$1,409,227	$4,284,148	$3,319,292
Investment Income	$2,870,173	$4,973,628	$6,755,242	$7,282,890
Pretax Profits from Underwriting and Investments	**$888,692**	**$6,382,855**	**$11,039,390**	**$10,602,182**

The insurance float of Berkshire consistently grew in the 1970's, from $42.9 million[8] in 1970 to $231.1 million in 1979.[9] Float compounded at a rate of 20.6% over the entire period. The float only cost Berkshire money in three of the 10 years, as underwriting produced a profit in the other seven years.[10] This means that Berkshire was able to get paid to borrow this money for seven years, and then only had to pay a low interest rate on the float in the other three years. This was a very attractive source of funds, and helped fuel the growth of the organization.

	1970	1974	1979
Loss Reserves	$29,758,739	$72,761,097	$197,698,000
Unearned Premiums	$17,482,957	$21,704,867	$73,604,000
Agents' Balances (Asset)	-$4,072,027	-$9,583,769	-$20,546,000
Reinsurance Recoverable (Asset)	-$304,400	-$2,459,093	-$5,965,000
Deferred Acquisition Cost	-	-$4,400,000	-$13,652,000
Total Float	**$42,865,269**	**$78,023,102**	**$231,138,000**
Float CAGR		16.2%	24.3%

While insurance was the dominant force behind Berkshire's profitability in the early 1970's, the results were volatile. Profitability turned downward in the mid 1970's, and the insurance group reported a pretax loss of $2.3 million in 1975.[11] The underwriting loss was due to an increase in the loss ratio, as the expense ratio only increased slightly.[12] This means that the company charged too low of rates on its policies.

	1971	1975	1979
Premiums Earned	$60,867,000	$58,336,000	$181,949,000
Total Losses and Expenses	$59,458,000	$68,983,000	$178,207,000
Pretax Underwriting Profit (Loss)	**$1,409,000**	**-$10,647,000**	**$3,742,000**

	Loss Ratio	**Expense Ratio**	**Combined Ratio***
1971	67.0%	30.1%	97.1%
1972	62.0%	29.7%	91.7%
1973	62.0%	32.5%	94.5%
1974	77.8%	32.0%	109.8%
1975	81.0%	34.4%	115.4%

*Includes Statutory Figures

The cost structure of Berkshire's insurance group meant that the expense ratio couldn't fall too much below 30%. This was due to the fact that the business had to pay commissions and brokerage expenses to agents in order to earn revenue. GEICO was able to achieve an expense ratio around half of Berkshire's because of their direct marketing strategy. Commissions and brokerage expenses made up 76.7% and 67.3% of Berkshire's underwriting expenses in 1978 and 1979, respectively.[13] Berkshire operated a lean insurance business, but the company would have to continue paying commissions as long as it continued under the same distribution method.

Underwriting Expense	1978	1979
Commissions and Brokerage	76.7%	67.3%
Salaries and Other Compensation	10.6%	12.7%
Taxes, Licenses, and Fees	7.4%	5.9%
Other Underwriting Expenses	11.2%	13.7%
Deferred Acquisition Costs	-6.0%	0.3%
Total Underwriting Expense	**100.0%**	**100.0%**

Luckily for shareholders, the underwriting losses in 1974 and 1975 were not a problem because Berkshire had multiple streams of earnings by this time. Illinois National earned $3.5 million in 1975, and Berkshire's portion of Blue Chip earned $2.2 million.[14] Even the textile business earned $1.7 million pretax that year, as the segment enjoyed a temporary upswing in results.[15] The stock market experienced a significant decline in 1973 and 1974, leading to some realized losses in the investment portfolio.[16]

Pretax Income	1971	1972	1973	1974	1975
Insurance	$6,732,000	$10,701,000	$10,249,000	$892,000	-$2,327,000
Textiles	$233,000	$1,697,000	$2,837,000	$2,660,000	$1,715,000
Banking	$2,192,000	$2,700,000	$2,782,000	$4,093,000	$3,450,000
Blue Chip Stamps	$68,000	$142,000	$1,124,000	$1,164,000	$2,172,000
Interest and Corporate Overhead	-$648,000	-$770,000	-$1,966,000	-$2,324,000	-$2,268,000
Realized Investment Gain	$1,028,000	$1,359,000	$1,331,000	-$1,908,000	-$2,888,000
Total Pretax Income	**$9,605,000**	**$15,829,000**	**$16,357,000**	**$4,577,000**	**-$146,000**

> "The paper record looked terrible, yet the future, what you might call the intrinsic record, the real business momentum, was gaining all the while."
> -Charlie Munger, *The Snowball*[17]

While the underlying businesses of Berkshire and Blue Chip were steadily expanding throughout the 1970's, the stock price was volatile. Buffett shut down his partnership, BPL, at the end of 1969. Partners of BPL received their proportion of Berkshire stock. By 1974, five years later, the stock price had gone nowhere.[18] However, plenty of value was created over that five year period. At the end of 1969, Berkshire had total equity of $43.9 million and earned operating profits of $4.3 million before realized gains on investments.[19] The total equity of Berkshire grew to $88.2 million by 1974, while the company earned $8.4 million that year before realized losses on the sale of investments.[20] Berkshire diversified away from the poor textile business by 1974, and the intrinsic value of the corporation was much higher than it was in 1969.

Berkshire owned stocks with a carrying value on the balance sheet of $28.7 million in 1972, with $11.3 million of that value invested in Blue Chip Stamps.[21] The Blue Chip Stamps stock was accounted for as an equity method investment on the balance sheet by 1973. These stocks had a market value of $31.8 million at the end of 1972.[22] As previously mentioned, Berkshire increased the capital of its insurance businesses in 1973 through the use of debt. Most of the capital in its insurance businesses was invested in common stocks. Due to this, Berkshire's common stock portfolio increased in 1973 to $63.5 million based on carrying value. However, Berkshire's portfolio experienced a decline in market value in 1973, ending the year down 18.4%.[23] The portfolio's value was down 37% below its cost at the end of 1974.[24]

The overall market fared much worse over that time period. The S&P 500 decreased 41.9% from 1972 to 1974.[25] With hindsight, we can see that Berkshire owned some extremely valuable businesses within the portfolio.

The market was just temporarily going through a difficult period at the time. Berkshire's investment in Affiliated Publications, the owner of the Boston Globe, was down 39.2% at the time.[26] Its newspaper dominated the Boston market, and the company was selling for a bargain price. The Washington Post, another newspaper that dominated its market, was down 24.7%.[27] Newspapers in general were good businesses during this time period, but newspapers that dominated large markets were among the best businesses in the world. Blue Chip Stamps, which Berkshire controlled, was down 59.5% below cost.[28] This was an incredible bargain.

> "You can argue that if you're not willing to react with equanimity to a market price decline of 50% two or three times a century, you're not fit to be a common shareholder and you deserve the mediocre result you're going to get compared to the people who do have the temperament and can be more philosophical about these market fluctuations."
> -Charlie Munger, BBC Interview[29]

The Washington Post Company

The Washington Post was started in 1877 in Washington D.C. Eugene Meyer bought the paper in 1933, and ownership of the paper stayed within his family until 2013. Katharine Graham, the daughter of Eugene Meyer, took control of the paper in 1963. The company had been privately held until its initial public offering in 1971 on the American Stock Exchange.[30]

The Washington Post Company operated the newspaper under the same name, but the company owned additional businesses as well. At the time of the initial public offering, the Washington Post owned Newsweek magazine, three television stations, and two radio stations. These were valuable assets.[31]

The Washington Post went public at a very difficult point in time. The company's public offering took place on June 15, 1971, while its newspaper began publishing the Pentagon Papers on June 18th of that year.[32] The decision to publish the Pentagon Papers was very controversial. Most executives who manage public corporations would try to avoid publicity like this around the time of a public offering. Investors in the early 1970's would have faced uncertainty surrounding potential repercussions to the Washington Post Company stemming from this decision.

In 1972, there was a breakin at the Watergate Complex. This led to another investigation by the Washington Post that received scrutiny. The company had licenses to operate television stations in Florida, and the licenses were up for renewal. It was not clear at the time if the government would allow the company to keep these licenses. Under normal circumstances, existing television stations had no problem renewing their license. These licenses had to be renewed every few years. Based on White House recordings, it is now clear that the Nixon administration was attempting to fight back against the Washington Post for its Watergate coverage by challenging the renewal of the license.[33] In the 1970's, investors would be faced with the uncertainty surrounding an important revenue stream for the Washington Post Company.

On top of the public scrutiny facing this public corporation, the overall stock market suffered declines in 1973 and 1974. The S&P 500 fell 41.9% from $118.05 in 1972 to $68.56 in 1974.[34] All of these circumstances led to a depressed stock price for the Washington Post in the 1970's. In its first year as a publicly traded company, the Washington Post had a market value of between $75.5 million and $103.7 million.[35] In 1972, the stock reached a high of $38 per share, valuing the company at $180.8 million. The company earned $11.8 million the year before, which was a 6.5% yield based on the firm's valuation at the time.[36] As the overall market declined, the stock price dropped 61.2% to a low of $14.75 in 1974. This valued the company at $70.1 million.[37] The company earned $13.3 million in 1973, amounting to 19% based on the 1974 valuation.[38]

The company's newspaper had the highest market share in the Washington D.C. area, with daily circulation reaching 523,201 in 1972 and Sunday circulation of 694,055.[39] The closest competitor in 1972 had daily circulation of 391,633 that year.[40] Newspapers were generally a

147

winner-take-all type of industry, and the company received national publicity for its investigations in the early 1970's. These two factors made it extremely unlikely that a competitor would knock off the Washington Post from its top spot in D.C. The firm's television stations had licenses in their local areas. While the stations still faced competition, government regulation meant that the businesses would be protected from a certain amount of pressure from new entrants. Newsweek, the company's magazine, might not have had quite as strong of competitive advantages as the firm's other businesses. However, the magazine had a recognizable brand name. The magazine business also produced a large amount of deferred revenue from subscriptions, which was beneficial for the funding of working capital.

Berkshire invested in the Washington Post in 1973, and paid $22.75 per share for its stake in the business. The position cost $10.6 million, and it meant that Berkshire owned close to 10% of the company. The stock represented 17% of Berkshire's portfolio at the time.[41] The stock price of the Washington Post hit a low of $14.75 in 1974, which meant that Berkshire's investment was down 35.2% in a short period of time. The price that Berkshire paid valued the Washington Post at $108 million.[42] The company earned $9.7 million in the prior year, which would have been a yield of 9% based on Berkshire's purchase price.[43] The company earned net income of $7.6 million on average over the previous six years, or 7% of the valuation based on Berkshire's purchase price.[44] The 10 year Treasury rate was 6.7% in 1973, so the Washington Post would yield a higher rate to Berkshire even if there was zero growth in the future.[45] As it turned out, there would be plenty of growth at the Washington Post.

Over the next decade, revenue compounded at a rate of 13.5% per year, from $246.9 million[46] in 1973 to $877.7 million in 1983.[47] Net income increased at a compound annual growth rate of 17.8%, from $13.3 million to $68.4 million over the same period. The Washington Post had a net profit margin of 5.4% in 1973, but this improved to 7.8% in 1983. The growth was all across the board for the company throughout the decade. Broadcasting revenues compounded at a rate of 15.9% per year, while the newspaper and

148

magazine segments experienced compound annual growth rates of 15.1% and 10.9%, respectively.[48]

The Washington Post used its strong cash flow to make acquisitions, as well as to repurchase its own stock. The company added to its newspaper segment through the acquisition of the Trenton Times in 1974,[49] and the Everett Herald in 1978.[50] Stanley H. Kaplan Educational Centers was acquired in 1984, and Kaplan became a very profitable company in the education field.[51] The Washington Post Company eventually invested in cable television as well.

The company repurchased significant amounts of stock during this period. In 1972, the company had 18,985,312 shares outstanding after adjusting for stock splits in 1976 and 1978.[52] By 1985, the number of shares outstanding dropped to 12,821,773.[53] This meant that continuing shareholders, like Berkshire, saw their ownership in the Washington Post increase without having to put up any additional money. Berkshire owned about 10% of the company in 1973, but this ownership increased to 13.5% of the company in 1985.[54] The Washington Post spent $233.8 million on share repurchases from 1973 to 1985. At the end of 1985, Berkshire's $10.6 million investment in the Washington Post Company had grown to $205.2 million.[55] With Berkshire's total equity amounting to $1.9 billion in 1985, this investment had become 10.9% of the company's book value.[56]

Nebraska Furniture Mart

By the 1980's, Berkshire Hathaway was a diversified conglomerate. The company had fully owned businesses involved in insurance, candy retailing, apparel retailing, furniture retailing, automotive chemical manufacturing, and publishing. Additionally, Berkshire had interests in many more industries through the partially owned businesses within the marketable securities portfolio. The firm continued to retain its earnings, and this led to compound interest working its magic. In 1983, Berkshire made an acquisition to add to the growing list of subsidiaries.

149

Berkshire acquired the Nebraska Furniture Mart in September 1983.[57] The founder, Rose Blumkin, and her family retained ownership of 10% of the business and had the option to buy back another 10%.[58] This option was eventually exercised, leaving Berkshire with 80% of the Nebraska Furniture Mart. Berkshire paid $55 million for its 80% share, valuing the entire business at $68.75 million.[59] This acquisition was small relative to Berkshire at the time, as the total amount of assets on the balance sheet for Berkshire amounted to $1.9 billion at the end of 1983. Berkshire's total equity was $1.1 billion that year.[60] Berkshire's share of the earnings amounted to $5.9 million in 1984, which was an initial yield of 10.8% based on the purchase price.[61] Berkshire reported net income of $148.9 million in 1984, so the Nebraska Furniture Mart made up just 4% of total earnings.[62] However, this was a business with a strong competitive position that would strengthen and further diversify Berkshire's earning power.

"Its store in Omaha, Nebraska is believed by Berkshire management to be the largest single furniture retail store in the United States. It has sizeable warehousing facilities near its retail outlet permitting it to serve a trade area within a radius of about 300 miles from Omaha."
-1983 Berkshire Hathaway Annual Report

The Nebraska Furniture Mart was a private business prior to the acquisition, so there is a limited amount of financial data available. However, the annual reports of Berkshire in the 1980's provide a glimpse into the business. The Nebraska Furniture Mart sold products at extremely low prices, as its gross margins were only slightly above 22.2% in 1984.[63] The business was able to sell at such a low margin because its operating expenses were so low. The Nebraska Furniture Mart had operating expenses of 16.5% of sales in 1984, resulting in a little over 5.7% of sales leftover as profit. Levitz Furniture, one of the largest direct competitors, had gross margins of 44.4% and operating expenses of 35.6% of its sales.[64] The efficient operations at the Nebraska Furniture Mart allowed the business to sell products at lower prices than its competition. Although the business had low margins, the increase in inventory turnover led to very good returns on capital. Additionally, establishing a business as the low cost operator creates a competitive advantage that is hard to disrupt. New entrants would be either unable or unwilling to compete with prices so low. This meant that Berkshire could expect cash profits to continue decades into the future.

> "In its fiscal 1984 10-K, the largest independent specialty retailer of home furnishings in the country, Levitz Furniture, described its prices as "generally lower than the prices charged by conventional furniture stores in its trading area". Levitz, in that year, operated at a gross margin of 44.4% (that is, on average, customers paid it $100 for merchandise that had cost it $55.60 to buy). The gross margin at NFM is not much more than half of that. NFM's low mark-ups are possible because of its exceptional efficiency: operating expenses (payroll, occupancy, advertising, etc.) are about 16.5% of sales versus 35.6% at Levitz."
> -Warren Buffett's 1984 Letter to Berkshire Hathaway Shareholders

Walmart - 1984		
Sales	$4,666,909,000	99.2%
Rentals from licensed departments	$10,175,000	0.2%
Other income	$25,856,000	0.5%
Total Revenues	**$4,702,940,000**	**100.0%**
COGS	$3,418,025,000	72.7%
Operating, SG&A	$892,887,000	19.0%
Debt	$4,935,000	0.1%
Capital Leases	$29,946,000	0.6%
Income before tax	**$357,147,000**	**7.6%**
Income tax	$160,903,000	3.4%
Net Income	**$196,244,000**	**4.2%**

Walmart provides for another interesting comparison. While the company was involved in more areas of retailing than the Nebraska Furniture Mart, the company was an extremely efficient operator and offered low prices to customers. Walmart had gross margins of 27.3% in 1984, and achieved operating expenses of just 19.7%.[65] The figures were even lower for the Nebraska Furniture Mart on both metrics. Operating expenses as a percentage of sales, for example, were 3.2% lower for the Nebraska Furniture Mart than for Walmart. Part of this was related to the financial structure of the Nebraska Furniture Mart. The company owned its locations and had no debt. Interest expense for Walmart, as well as rent paid on operating leases, amounted to 2.1% of sales. Walmart was a low cost operator back in 1984 just as it is today. With that being said, its low prices were no match for the Nebraska Furniture Mart at the time.

1984	NFM	Walmart	Levitz
Gross Margin	22.2%*	27.3%	44.4%
Operating Expenses	16.5%	19.7%	35.6%
Profit Margin	5.7%	7.6%	8.8%

*Disclosed as 'not much more than' 22.2% in the 1984 Letter to Shareholders

Berkshire Hathaway

At the end of 1978, Diversified Retailing was merged into Berkshire.[66] Diversified Retailing owned Associated Retail Stores, which was a retailer of apparel. The company was also involved in the insurance business through its Columbia Insurance and Southern Casualty subsidiaries. Diversified Retailing owned 16% of the stock of Blue Chip as well, so Berkshire was able to increase its ownership in the company through this merger.[67] This led to the results of Blue Chip to be consolidated within Berkshire's financial statements for the first time in 1978.

> "Prior to the aforesaid merger, subsidiaries of Diversified owned approximately 16% of the outstanding stock of Blue Chip Stamps ("Blue Chip"), while at the same time The Registrant and its subsidiaries owned approximately 41% of such outstanding stock; the combination of these holdings resulting from the merger caused Blue Chip to become an approximately 58% owned subsidiary of The Registrant."
> -1978 Berkshire Hathaway Annual Report

By the 1980's, See's Candy had established itself as a very critical piece of Berkshire. In 1982, See's made up a quarter of Berkshire's total revenues and more than half of its pretax operating profits.[68] The candy retailer enjoyed quite a bit of growth since it was acquired, and the business was able to pay out a material amount of cash to Berkshire and Blue Chip. Buffett and Munger were then able to reinvest this cash elsewhere.

While See's was important to Berkshire's success, insurance was still the company's backbone. The insurance segment consistently was the leader in terms of revenue, but also provided Berkshire with important investment income. Premiums earned at Berkshire grew from $20.5 million[69] in 1967 to $186.1 million in 1978, which was a 22.2% compound annual growth rate.[70] However, the growth slowed in the early 1980's. Berkshire earned premiums of $140.2 million in 1984, 24.6% below the 1978 figure.[71] The company had plenty of capital to write premiums, but the industry was just not offering profitable underwriting. Berkshire had total equity of $1.3 billion.[72] It would have been quite normal for companies within the industry to write premiums that were twice as high as their equity value. In Berkshire's case, this would have meant premiums of $2.6 billion in 1984. The insurance group of Berkshire was extremely under leveraged during this time period and it had the potential to grow the business if profitable underwriting became available.

The degree to which Berkshire was under leveraged was unique in the insurance industry for reasons relating to both the balance sheet and the income statement. On the balance sheet side, few companies have retained earnings like Berkshire. Most companies pay out dividends to shareholders instead of reinvesting everything back into the business. When companies do retain earnings, few are able to earn such high rates on their incremental investments as Berkshire had. Berkshire compounded its total equity by 24.2% per year from 1965 to 1985, which led to the company overflowing with capital. On the income statement side, not many managers would be willing to accept reductions in premiums when so much capital was available. Berkshire was more patient and disciplined than usual, which allowed for periods of declining premiums in its insurance business. Additionally, Berkshire was not tied to one industry. The company was opportunistic in terms of its investments, and this led to diversified earning power. When premiums were reduced at the insurance group, Berkshire still had profits rolling in from See's Candy and other subsidiaries. This diversified stream of earnings allowed for more flexibility at Berkshire.

The cost structure of most firms within the industry also allows for reductions in revenue. An insurance business incurs expenses from losses on policies, as well as costs from overhead. If an insurance company had zero sales, then there would be no losses on policies. No commissions or brokerage expenses would need to be paid if sales were zero. Berkshire reported other underwriting expenses of $11.8 million in 1978 and $18.9 million in 1979.[73] The company had total equity of $345 million in 1979, so Berkshire could have handled a long period of zero premiums within its insurance group.[74] See's Candy alone would have been able to absorb most of the overhead of the insurance operation, as See's earned $12.8 million pretax in 1979.[75]

Underwriting Expense	1978	1979
Commissions and Brokerage	$38,977,000	$38,966,000
Salaries and Other Compensation	$5,394,000	$7,321,000
Taxes, Licenses, and Fees	$3,751,000	$3,435,000
Other Underwriting Expenses	$5,681,000	$7,954,000
Deferred Acquisition Costs	-$2,994,000	$194,000
Total Underwriting Expenses	**$50,809,000**	**$57,870,000**

The investment income was always a crucial aspect of Berkshire's insurance business. By 1984 the importance was even more clear. The specialized auto and general liability segment led the way for the insurance group of Berkshire with $88.4 million of premiums earned in 1980. The Home State companies earned premiums of $43.1 million that year, while the reinsurance segment earned $33.8 million. Berkshire recorded investment income of $31.1 million in 1980.[76] However, the tables were turned in 1984. Investment income registered $69.3 million, while the largest insurance segment only earned premiums of $64 million.[77] It is rare for the investment income of an insurance company to outpace its own sales of insurance policies, but that was the situation for Berkshire in 1984.

Premiums Earned	1980	1982	1984
Specialized Auto and General Liability	$88,404,000	$69,026,000	$64,003,000
Workers Compensation	$19,890,000	$15,951,000	$22,665,000
Home State Multiple Lines	$43,089,000	$37,552,000	$32,598,000
Reinsurance	$33,804,000	$27,408,000	$16,066,000
Structured Settlements and Portfolio Reinsurance	-	$3,008,000	$4,910,000
Total Premiums	**$185,187,000**	**$152,945,000**	**$140,242,000**
Investment income	$31,111,000	$41,791,000	$69,281,000
Total Insurance Revenues	**$216,298,000**	**$194,736,000**	**$209,523,000**

Berkshire was sitting on some serious unrealized gains in the 1980's. The portfolio had unrealized gains of $135 million in 1980 after accounting for taxes, which was 34.2% of the total $395.2 million equity value.[78] By 1985, the after-tax value of unrealized gains increased to $664.7 million. The unrealized gains accounted for 35.3% of the $1.8 billion of total equity in 1985.[79] On a pretax basis, Berkshire had unrealized gains of $923 million in 1985. GEICO accounted for 59.6% of this gain, or $550.2 million. The Washington Post Company, another long term holding for Berkshire, accounted for 21.2% of the unrealized gain or $195.4 million.[80]

156

Stocks - 1985	Cost	Market	Unrealized Gain
Affiliated Publications	$3,516,000	$55,710,000	$52,194,000
American Broadcasting Companies	$54,435,000	$108,997,000	$54,562,000
Beatrice Companies	$106,811,000	$108,142,000	$1,331,000
GEICO Corporation	$45,713,000	$595,950,000	$550,237,000
Handy & Harman	$27,318,000	$43,718,000	$16,400,000
Time, Inc	$20,385,000	$52,669,000	$32,284,000
The Washington Post Company	$9,731,000	$205,172,000	$195,441,000
All Other Common Stockholdings	$7,201,000	$27,963,000	$20,762,000
Total Common Stocks	**$275,110,000**	**$1,198,321,000**	**$923,211,000**

The book value of Berkshire increased by $1.5 billion from 1980 to 1985. An increase of $805.9 million was attributable to retained earnings, while $529.7 million was attributable to the after-tax value of unrealized gains on marketable securities. However, taxes would not have to be paid on the gains from marketable securities until they were realized. Berkshire owned some stocks for decades, which deferred taxes for a long period of time.

The main reason that Berkshire was able to have the cash to invest in marketable securities was due to its growth in float. From 1980 to 1985, float compounded at a rate of 17.4% annually. Float grew from $230.8 million[81] in 1980 to $514.9 million in 1985.[82] Very few insurance companies could achieve the growth in float that Berkshire did. Even if other insurance companies could find profitable underwriting, at some point they would end up with too much operating leverage. Berkshire had plenty of capital because it earned such high returns on its investments, and then retained all of its earnings. Not many portfolio managers could match the returns that Buffett and Munger achieved. Few companies neglected dividend payments to retain earnings as well.

	1980	1985
Losses and Loss Adjustment Expense	$199,128,000	$411,305,000
Unearned Premiums	$73,281,000	$229,440,000
Agents' Balances (Asset)	-$21,759,000	-$74,001,000
Reinsurance Recoverable	-$5,665,000	-$490,000
Deferred Acquisition Cost	-$14,163,000	-$51,368,000
Total Float	**$230,822,000**	**$514,886,000**
Float CAGR		17.4%

X. The Conclusion

Acquire Great Businesses, Not Bargains

An enormous amount of wealth was created by Berkshire. However, the decision Buffett made to originally invest in Berkshire was a mistake. Although the rate of return of Berkshire's stock price is legendary for a public company, it does not validate Buffett's original investment decision.

Berkshire made significant changes to allocate capital away from textiles during the 1960's and 1970's. However, the original textile business still weighed down the overall results at Berkshire over this period. When Buffett took control of Berkshire, the firm's capital was completely within the textile business. By 1970, only about a quarter of the capital of Berkshire was tied up in the textile operations.[1] This dropped to just under 10% by 1978.[2] The textile operations lost money in 1970, and earned $1.3 million in 1978 on capital of about $17 million.[3] The textile operation was finally closed down in 1985.[4]

The textile segment of Berkshire averaged pretax profits of $1.3 million during the 1970's. This business segment averaged a loss of $1.1 million from 1980 to 1985. The average return on equity for the textile segment from 1970 to 1985 was not much more than 1%. While still not great, the average return on equity had a better run during the 1970's. From 1970 to 1979, the textile operations averaged a return on equity of about 6%. Berkshire achieved much better returns from its other investments though. The insurance group within Berkshire averaged a return on equity of 13.6% during the 1970's, while Illinois National averaged 15.8% from 1970 to 1978. Associated Cotton, which Buffett owned through the Diversified Retailing Company, typically earned around 20% on capital.[5] Instead of purchasing these businesses through Berkshire, Buffett could have acquired them directly. Over time, the result would have been drastic due to the ability to compound capital at higher rates.

> "Textile plant and equipment are on the books for a very small fraction of what it would cost to replace such equipment today. And, despite the age of the equipment, much of it is functionally similar to new equipment being installed by the industry. But despite this "bargain cost" of fixed assets, capital turnover is relatively low reflecting required high investment levels in receivables and inventory compared to sales. Slow capital turnover, coupled with low profit margins on sales, inevitably produces inadequate returns on capital."
> -Warren Buffett's 1978 Letter to Berkshire Hathaway Shareholders

Although its return on equity was already low, the reality of the textile business' economics was worse than it might appear on the surface. As Buffett explained to shareholders in his 1978 letter, textile assets on the balance sheet were reported at values far below replacement cost. This was due to the accumulated depreciation on those assets, as well as Berkshire's prudence in keeping expenditures low for new plant equipment. If the business was to continue many years into the future, then eventually these assets would need to be replaced. The already unimpressive return on equity would be reduced under this scenario.

While the return on equity was overstated for the textile operations, the opposite was true for the insurance business. The insurance group within Berkshire had significant unrealized gains on equity securities. These gains did not show up in the reported net income number until they were actually realized. This was the main reason why Berkshire was able to compound its equity at a larger rate than what showed up in the return on equity figure.

Buffett initially invested in Berkshire at $7.51 per share in 1962,[6] but paid an average of $14.86 per share in order to take control in 1965.[7] However, he added to the position over the next handful of years. In early 1966, BPL owned 54.3% of Berkshire.[8] Shortly after the National Indemnity acquisition, BPL's ownership increased to 64.7%.[9] From 1965 to 1985, the value of Berkshire increased from $16.9 million to $3.1 billion.[10] This means that by 1985 Buffett created $1.1 billion of wealth for the people who owned the other 35.3% of Berkshire. All of the increase in value came from businesses

161

other than the original textile operation. Instead of buying the Berkshire stock that appeared cheap, Buffett or BPL could have directly acquired high quality businesses and owned them outright. Before shutting down the partnership in the late 1960's, BPL had assets of over $100 million.[11] With this money, Buffett could have bought all of National Indemnity, Illinois National, Associated Retailing, and had money to spare. At one time, BPL owned 5% of both Disney[12] and American Express.[13]

American Express specifically provides an interesting case study. BPL invested heavily in American Express in the mid 1960's, with the initial purchase taking place sometime near the end of 1963. The stock eventually accounted for around 40% of the assets of the partnership.[14] BPL wasn't the only vehicle that Buffett used to invest in American Express though. Berkshire Hathaway itself also owned shares in this financial powerhouse.

American Express

Berkshire Hathaway first disclosed a position in American Express in its 1967 annual report, which had a fiscal year end of September 30th that year. At the time, Berkshire owned 15,000 shares of American Express at a cost of $1.1 million or $71 per share.[15] The stock price was between $66.13 and $94.50 in 1966, but never dropped below $89.25 in 1967.[16] The previous annual report did not list American Express in its portfolio, which means the investment was probably made sometime between September and December of 1966. It is interesting that Buffett started buying the stock through BPL at close to $35 per share, but was still willing to pay close to twice as much for it three years later.[17] Berkshire still owned all of these shares at the end of 1968, after adjusting for stock splits.[18] At cost, the American Express stock accounted for about 2.8% of Berkshire's assets in 1967,[19] and between 4.9% and 6.1% of Berkshire's market capitalization that year.[20]

> "Founded in a day of relatively primitive transportation and communication, for the purpose of transporting gold, silver, currency, commercial paper and small articles of value between New York and Buffalo, American Express filled a basic need in the expanding world of commerce and industry. As time passed, new needs were met and additional services were developed, until 101 years later, the words "American Express" mean an international network of offices offering travel, financial and foreign shipping services for a variety of personal and business needs."
>
> -American Express 1951 Annual Report

Although the company began in 1850 in the express business, delivering mail and other goods across the country, American Express started selling money orders in 1882.[21] The first Travelers Cheque was cashed in 1891.[22] The company eventually expanded into several other businesses, including the credit card by 1958.[23]

In the early 1960's, American Express was a company that was firing on all cylinders. Both sales and profits were growing rapidly, and the company had developed a valuable brand over many decades. The company's products relied on the trust of consumers and merchants, and the market share of American Express proved that the brand was trusted.

American Express had a large network of office branches in the U.S. and abroad, with 423 offices in total in 1965.[24] The company also developed strong relationships with banks that sold American Express products, leading to 84,234 other American Express selling outlets.[25] This helped bring recognition and accessibility to the American Express brand, but it was not the only reason for the brand's value. The American Express brand earned its value by being reliable during some of the most painful moments in the 1900's. When the First World War initially broke out, as well as during the Bank Holiday of 1933 in the U.S., many banks refused to serve customers in order to prevent runs. However, customers were still able to cash American Express Money Orders and Travelers Cheques.[26] In both cases, the products of American Express proved more reliable than the currency of the U.S. and of large European nations. Customers and merchants could rely on American Express to complete transactions during a period of extreme panic, and this proved to have a lasting effect on the minds of customers all over the world.

Operating revenue and net income increased every single year from 1950 to 1965. American Express grew operating revenue at a compound annual growth rate of 12.8%, from $23.6 million[27] in 1950 to $143.4 million in 1965.[28] Net income went from $3 million to $15.6 million or 11.6% compounded annually over the same period. The company had double digit profit margins over the entire period, achieving 10.6% in its worst year. Other than in 1950 and 1951, the return on equity was in the double digits each year and was steadily trending upward. This is evidence that American Express was a strong and consistent business.

At $71 per share in 1966, American Express was selling for $331.7 million.[27] This valuation would give investors in American Express an initial yield of 4.7% based on profits of $15.6 million reported in the most recent annual report from 1965.[28] This was pretty close to the 4.8% rate on the 10 year treasury bond at the end of that year.[29] This means that investors could obtain a similar initial yield whether they invested in treasury bonds or in American Express stock, assuming profits could remain at historical levels. Investors would have to take on business risks with American Express, but they would also receive the benefit if the company could grow at all, like it had done consistently in the past.

Although American Express had many business segments, the two most important by far were the American Express Credit Card and the company's Travelers Cheques. Both businesses had attractive economics, and had dominant positions compared to their competitors. The Travelers Cheque captured 60% market share in the 1960's, up from 50% in the 1920's.[30] The American Express Credit Card was started in late 1958, and lost money for the first three years. However, the card started to produce a profit in 1962.[31] The credit card had high growth in both the number of cardholders as well as the dollar value spent by each cardholder. This growth was accelerating in the mid 1960's.

164

	Cardholders	Total Billings	Establishments*
1959	700,000	$75,000,000	41,455
1960	785,000	$120,000,000	46,982
1961	825,000	$152,000,000	50,676
1962	890,000	$189,000,000	81,989
1963	1,020,000	$242,000,000	85,000
1964	1,225,000	$344,000,000	121,000
1965	1,580,000	$556,000,000	128,000

Growth Rate	Cardholders	Total Billings	Establishments*
1960	12.1%	60.0%	13.3%
1961	5.1%	26.7%	7.9%
1962	7.9%	24.3%	61.8%
1963	14.6%	28.0%	3.7%
1964	20.1%	42.1%	42.4%
1965	29.0%	61.6%	5.8%

*The number of establishments that accepted the American Express Credit Card

In addition to growth, the credit card showed evidence of having pricing power. American Express charged an annual fee to cardholders, and also charged merchants a percentage of all transactions paid for with the credit card. In 1961, American Express raised the annual fee from $6 to $8, but the number of cardholders still grew.[32] The company also increased the charge to merchants that year, but the number of establishments accepting the credit card increased. Soon after, the annual charge was raised to $10, but the credit card kept growing at an even faster rate.[33] It is nice to be able to raise your prices and still have growth all around the board.

American Express received fees of 3.75% on each transaction by 1976.[34] Many business owners would enjoy receiving a few percent each time someone swiped a credit card. If the amount charged to merchants in the 1960's was between 2% to 3%, then that would produce revenues for

165

American Express of $11.1 million to $16.7 million in 1965. With about 1.6 million cardholders, this would mean that the company was earning $15.8 million from the annual fee they received.

Another important business was the company's Travelers Cheques. The majority of Travelers Cheques were sold at banks. Customers would pay cash to the bank in exchange for these cheques, which came in handy for people who traveled or wanted to avoid carrying around large amounts of cash. American Express guaranteed replacement of lost or stolen cheques, and the cheques were accepted in most banks and places of business around the world.

The main source of profit from the cheques came from income received by investing the float. In this context, float was generated from the fact that American Express received cash immediately from customers, and wouldn't need to pay it back until the customer made a purchase at a later date. This timing difference provided a benefit that is similar to how insurance companies operate. The company charged other fees as well, but these were minimal compared to the income earned on investing the float. American Express would charge a small fee to customers who bought Travelers Cheques, but also had to pay a commission to the bank that distributed the cheques. In the 1956 annual report, American Express disclosed that they charged customers 1% fees on the sale of Travelers Cheques.

"On May 1, 1956 charges to the public for our Travelers Cheques were increased from 3/4% to 1% of the amount purchased."
-1956 American Express Annual Report

Travelers Cheques were usually outstanding for only a short period of time. Typically, there was a month or two from when a cheque was purchased until it was cashed.[35] At the individual cheque level, the company wouldn't be able to earn much of a return over this short time frame. However, the total liability for cheques outstanding was pretty consistent and reliable, so the company could invest in medium to long term bonds. For decades, the

166

liability on the balance sheet for Travelers Cheques continued to grow. This meant that sales of new Travelers Cheques consistently outpaced the redemption of old Travelers Cheques. In 1965, the company reported a $572.5 million liability for these Travelers Cheques outstanding.[36] In effect, American Express was able to borrow this amount of money from its customers without having to pay any interest. The company effectively earned interest to borrow this money due to the small sales charge customers paid. The catch was that customers at any time, through spending their cheques, could demand that American Express pay back the loan in full. The company never experienced any major wave of net redemptions, and the outstanding amount of Travelers Cheques grew every single year from 1950 to 1965, with a compound annual growth rate of 7.6% over that period.

	Travelers Cheque Liability	Growth	CAGR Since 1950
1950	190,259,532		
1955	282,832,209	48.7%	8.3%
1960	365,525,914	29.2%	6.7%
1965	572,457,965	56.6%	7.6%

Within Blue Chip Stamps, as well as within the insurance businesses of Berkshire, Buffett invested float more aggressively and less conventionally than the competition. If BPL was able to take a controlling stake in American Express, it could have used the float to buy stocks or entire businesses, just as Berkshire and Blue Chip had done. However, the weight of a low return textile business would not be weighing down the results under this scenario.

American Express broke out its investments on the balance sheet. Even though these investments weren't strictly for the Travelers Cheque float, it still provides some insight into how the company handled investment of its assets. Common stocks had a value on the balance sheet of $15.5 million, which made up 2.6% of the total security investment assets in 1965.[37] National Indemnity invested 29% of its portfolio in stocks in 1965 prior to

167

being acquired by Berkshire.[38] By 1973, National Indemnity had 44.8% of its portfolio in stocks.[39] Since its insurance companies were regulated, Berkshire's portfolio allocation to stocks was dependent on how much equity capital the business had. Berkshire often had common stocks around a similar level to that of its equity, while bonds and cash offset policyholders' funds. American Express had less pressure regarding its portfolio allocation since it did not answer to insurance regulators. In 1965, American Express had equity of $93.8 million, but owned stocks of just $15.5 million.[40] An aggressive portfolio manager could have greatly increased the allocation of the portfolio to stocks at American Express.

Out of the $572.5 million float, if Buffett could have aggressively invested 25% of that and left the rest in safe, short-term bonds, the results would have been outstanding. Assuming he could have earned around 20% on this aggressively invested float, that would have produced $28.6 million in investment income. This is all on interest-free borrowed money. For normal mortals, 20% returns every year would be an outrageous assumption, but by 1966 Buffett had a long track record of outperforming this benchmark. Even if we tone down the rate of return assumptions, it is still a solid improvement. American Express had operating revenue of $143.4 million in 1965, so this hypothetical amount of investment income would have been meaningful if Buffett was able to produce it.

Berkshire Hathaway reached the $500 million level of float in 1985. Buffett could have reached this level two decades earlier in the 1960's with American Express. Also, it is fun to think about the possibilities Buffett could have had with this float in the early to mid 1970's. The stock market crashed in 1973 and 1974, so the value of the float probably would have dropped as well. However, great businesses were selling for some ridiculous prices. If Buffett had access to this kind of float in 1974, he might have been able to really make something of himself.

Over the few years Berkshire owned American Express, the stock went up 224.3%, or 3.24 times higher than its original cost.[41] Any other manager of a textile business would have earned low returns on this capital, but

Buffett put the capital to great use. By 1973, the stock went up almost 10 times higher than Berkshire's original cost, so Berkshire missed out on some of these gains. Berkshire ended up selling American Express and liquidating its portfolio of stocks in 1969 in order to buy the Illinois National Bank.

Stay Flexible, Avoid Biases

Throughout their careers, Buffett and Munger were incredibly open minded regarding opportunities that came along. While managing Berkshire, decisions were clearly made with the shareholders' best long term interests in mind. This is not the case at many corporations, as pressures mount to hit earnings targets each upcoming quarter. People yearn for conventionality, as it is safer to fail acting like everyone else than to fail taking an unconventional path. Berkshire acquired control of entire businesses in many circumstances, but made major investments where they had no control whatsoever. They were willing to report financial statements with fully consolidated investments, equity method investments and cost method investments. It did not matter if acquisitions resulted in profit to Berkshire's bottom line, or if the gain in value would go unreported on the income statement. They invested in a wide range of industries as well.

Buffett and Munger were excellent at avoiding commitment bias, and faced the facts regarding negative situations. They were not afraid to reverse course when things didn't go as planned. Many people face difficult situations with psychological denial. Buffett and Munger showed many examples of avoiding denial even when it would have been convenient.

Berkshire had a long history in the textile field. When Buffett took over, all of its capital was invested in textiles. Very quickly after taking over, Buffett changed the direction of Berkshire. While Buffett admitted that Berkshire remained in textiles for too long, at least the majority of the company's capital was reinvested into more productive areas.

Buffett, Munger, and Gottesman formed Diversified Retailing with the intention of making acquisitions in the retail field. A few years after making their first acquisition, Hochschild Kohn, they realized they made a mistake and sold the business. Diversified Retailing did make one beneficial acquisition, Associated Retailing, but that was about it. Not too long after forming Diversified Retailing, the company held one retailer and then some stocks. They bought the stock of Blue Chip Stamps as well as the stock of Berkshire. Diversified Retailing did incredibly well on these investments, but it was not the path that the company initially set out on.

After owning Wesco Financial for a period, management decided to get out of the savings and loan business. Wesco divested all of its banking business other than its home office. An unusual amount of capital was kept within Wesco, and the former S&L acquired multiple businesses outside of the finance industry.

The Success of Berkshire

In 1962, Buffett paid $7.51 per share for his initial purchase of Berkshire stock. In 1985, Berkshire reached a stock price of $2,730 per share.[42] The stock price of Berkshire was 363.5 times higher in 1985 than in 1962. This was a compound annual growth rate of 29.2%, while the S&P 500 only increased by 7.2% including dividends.[43] A $2,750 investment in Berkshire over this period would have grown to about $1 million by the end of 1985, compared to just $13,750 for an investor in the S&P 500. Berkshire was only worth $12.1 million at the beginning of the period. By the end of 1985, Berkshire was selling for $3.1 billion.

The stock price of Berkshire increased over time because the intrinsic value of the company genuinely increased. From Buffett's initial purchase in 1962 until the end of 1985, the stock price of Berkshire compounded at a rate of 29.2%. Over that same period, the total equity of the company reported on the balance sheet compounded at a rate of 19%. However, Berkshire also benefited because they went from selling for a discount to total equity in 1962 to selling at a premium in 1985. Buffett made his initial investment at 37.2% of total equity in 1962, while Berkshire traded for 166.1% of total equity in 1985.[44] This change makes sense given how different Berkshire was in 1962 compared to 1985. Berkshire went from a declining business earning low returns on capital, to a growing, diversified business earning high returns on capital.

Berkshire was able to compound its total equity at 19% per year. This means that total equity increased by $1.8 billion. Berkshire was able to accomplish this by earning good returns on capital while retaining just about all of its earnings. Appreciation in its marketable securities portfolio helped as well.

Berkshire earned low returns during the first few years after Buffett invested. Berkshire lost money in 1962 and 1963, and had a return on equity of just 0.8% in 1964.[45] However, Berkshire began to earn higher returns over time. From 1965 to 1969, Berkshire averaged a return on equity of just above 10%. From 1970 to 1975, Berkshire averaged returns on equity of 13.4%. The average return on equity increased to 20.4% from 1976 until 1985. These return on equity figures use the beginning total equity value in each year. As textiles became a smaller proportion of overall business, the returns increased at Berkshire. The improving return on equity achieved by Berkshire is made more impressive by the fact that the company's equity was growing rapidly. The company reinvested all of its earnings back into the business, with the exception of a small dividend in 1967.[46] If it had instead paid out an annual dividend, Berkshire would be much smaller and shareholders would be much poorer. Each additional dollar reinvested back into the business earned a correspondingly high rate of return. The total equity of Berkshire increased by $1.8 billion from 1962 to 1985. Over that time frame, Berkshire reported $1.1 billion of net income. The earnings Berkshire retained accounted for 58.9% of the increase in total equity.

Berkshire had a meaningful amount of unrealized gains on marketable securities. At the time, gains on marketable securities only showed up on the income statement when the gains were realized and the securities were sold. By the 1980's, stocks owned within the insurance group were reported at fair value on the balance sheet. This means that although unrealized gains on

171

marketable securities did not affect reported profits, the gains in value increased total equity on the balance sheet. When stocks were owned at the parent company or within a non-insurance business, the securities were reported on the balance sheet at the lower of cost or fair value. The marketable securities portfolio of Berkshire had unrealized gains of $664.7 million in 1985, net of tax.[47] The unrealized gains within the marketable securities portfolio, plus the retained earnings of Berkshire, minus the money Berkshire spent repurchasing its own stock accounts for the change in total equity over the period.

As the intrinsic value of Berkshire increased, so did the personal fortune of Buffett. For most of this period, Buffett was only paid a salary of about $50,000 as well as $18,000 in annual retirement benefits. In 1974, for example, Kenneth Chace was paid a salary of $79,576 and $35,000 in annual retirement benefits to run the textile operations.[48] By 1982, Buffett's salary was up to $100,000 per year.[49] Buffett did not receive stock options, as his ownership was purchased in the open market with his own capital. Buffett's wealth increased proportionally with all of the shareholders of Berkshire. He had as much skin in the game as possible. In 1971, about a year after BPL was discontinued, Buffett and his family owned 40.3% of Berkshire.[50] In 2006, Buffett announced that he would start donating large amounts of his fortune to charity.[51] At that point, he owned 32.3% of the company.[52] This amounted to 498,320 Class A shares of Berkshire stock.[53] At the end of 2019, these shares would represent ownership of 30.7% of Berkshire. The percentage of ownership declined slightly due to the dilution from acquisitions over the years. However, this level of ownership at the end of 2019 would amount to a staggering $169.2 billion. If Buffett never donated these Berkshire shares to charity, he would have been the richest person in the world at the end of 2019.

Berkshire was able to achieve this outstanding record while taking much less risk than usual. Risk is a complex subject and difficult to measure. The most common risk for businesses comes from issues with leverage. While it magnifies gains, leverage also magnifies losses. Leverage can be either financial or operational. Financial leverage comes in the form of debt, and operating leverage for insurance companies can be measured by comparing the amount of premiums to equity. Berkshire avoided much of either type of leverage.

Operating Leverage	Premiums Earned	Total Equity of Berkshire	Premiums/Equity
1970	$39,172,512	$48,483,333	80.8%
1975	$58,335,706	$92,890,192	62.8%
1980	$185,187,000	$395,214,000	46.9%
1985	$317,059,000	$1,885,330,000	16.8%

It is common for insurance companies to write more annual premiums than they have in equity. In some cases, premiums can reach two or three times higher than equity without raising too many red flags. From Berkshire's acquisition of National Indemnity in 1967 until 1985, the company only had one year in which premiums earned were above the parent company's total equity. Premiums were 108.4% of total equity in 1971.[54] In 1984, the premiums earned by Berkshire were only 11% of total equity.[55] American International Group, also known as AIG, earned premiums of 83.5% of its capital that same year.[56] On average, the ratio for Berkshire was closer to 50% from 1969 to 1985. Berkshire was unique in the sense that its equity was made up of many businesses outside of the insurance industry. However, the company was still under leveraged. This meant that Berkshire had plenty of equity capital to absorb losses from its insurance businesses if needed.

Financial Leverage	Total Debt	Total Equity of Berkshire	Debt/Equity
1970	$7,391,300	$48,483,333	15.2%
1975	$24,108,300	$92,890,192	26.0%
1980	$104,344,000	$395,214,000	26.4%
1985	$117,879,000	$1,885,330,000	6.3%

Berkshire also avoided burdening itself with too much financial leverage. From 1969 to 1985, Berkshire's debt to equity ratio reached a high of 36.9% in 1977.[57] The average over the period was below 20%. In 1985, Berkshire had debt of just 6.3% of equity.[58] Obviously a firm with little debt has less to worry about during an economic downturn. On the flip side, Berkshire still had the option to increase leverage and bring in added liquidity if it was needed. The lack of financial leverage provided additional flexibility to Berkshire over the years.

The top ten companies in the 1965 Fortune 500 are listed in the following table.[59] The table shows how these companies from 1965 fared in 2019. Standard Oil of New Jersey, which was number two on the list in 1965, later became Exxon. Number five on the list, Socony Mobil Oil, became known as Mobil and merged with Exxon to form Exxon Mobil. Chrysler was acquired by Fiat after going bankrupt. Texaco and Gulf Oil are both now part of Chevron. Berkshire's profits surpassed all of these companies, while only Exxon Mobil had higher revenues in 2019. Berkshire reported $81.5 billion in profits in 2019, which dwarfed every other company on this list. The next highest reported profit on the list was Exxon Mobil with $14.3 billion. However, the reported net income for Berkshire was not a true measure of their profitability for the year. 2019 was the second fiscal year in which their unrealized gains or losses on investments were counted within net income. Berkshire had unrealized gains on equity securities of $53.7 billion in 2019. The change in value of investments has a meaningful impact on Berkshire over the long term, but the year-to-year change is not important. Excluding the effect of unrealized gains on marketable securities, Berkshire would have reported income of $27.7 billion. While this number is much smaller for Berkshire than the reported net income figure, it still is almost double the amount of the second place company on the list, Exxon Mobil.

2019	Revenues (USD)	Profits (USD)*
General Motors	$137,237,000,000	$6,732,000,000
Standard Oil of New Jersey (Exxon Mobil)	$264,938,000,000	$14,340,000,000
Ford Motor	$155,900,000,000	$47,000,000
General Electric	$95,214,000,000	-$5,439,000,000
Mobil	Merged with Exxon	-
Chrysler (Fiat Chrysler)	$108,187,000,000	$6,622,000,000
U.S. Steel	$12,937,000,000	-$630,000,000
Texaco (Chevron)	$139,865,000,000	$2,924,000,000
International Business Machines	$77,147,000,000	$9,431,000,000
Gulf Oil	Merged with Chevron	-
Berkshire Hathaway	$256,100,000,000	$81,417,000,000

*Includes the effect of unrealized gains and losses on marketable securities

---

"One friendly but sharp−eyed commentator on Berkshire has pointed out that our book value at the end of 1964 would have bought about one−half ounce of gold and, fifteen years later, after we have plowed back all earnings along with much blood, sweat and tears, the book value produced will buy about the same half ounce. A similar comparison could be drawn with Middle Eastern oil. The rub has been that government has been exceptionally able in printing money and creating promises, but is unable to print gold or create oil."

-Warren Buffett's 1979 Letter to Berkshire Hathaway Shareholders

---

Although Berkshire created an incredible amount of value over this time period, the price of gold proved to be tough competition for a while. From

1965 to 1980, Berkshire's total equity compounded at a rate of 20.4% per year. Over this same time period, the price of gold compounded at 20.7% per year. Inflation was a difficult challenge during these years, which led to gold rising in price. In 1965, the 10 year treasury rate was 4.6%.[60] The rate was up to 12.8% by 1980.[61] The rate of inflation was at 1.6% in 1965, but moved up to 13.5% in 1980. The Consumer Price Index, a measure used to identify the rate of inflation, moved from 31.5 to 82.4 over the period for a compound annual growth rate of 6.6%.[62] While the nominal rate of return Berkshire earned on its equity was 20.4% per year, the real rate was around 13.8%. Most investors fared much worse. The S&P 500 only compounded at a rate of 5.1% from 1965 to 1980 including dividends.[63] This meant that investors in the S&P lost 1.5% per year in terms of actual purchasing power due to inflation over that time period.

While it may be tempting to look at the returns for gold from 1965 to 1980, these were abnormally good years for the commodity. Inflation was dramatically reduced in the early 1980's as Paul Volcker became chairman of the Federal Reserve. By 1985, the inflation rate was down to 3.5% after being at 13.5% in 1980.[64] The value of gold decreased by 45% over this five year period, while Berkshire continued to compound its total equity at high rates. Gold slightly outperformed Berkshire's total equity growth during the first 15 years of Buffett's tenure, but the next five years changed that completely. In the 20 year period from 1965 to 1985, Berkshire's total equity compounded at a rate of 24.2%, compared to an increase of 11.7% for gold. Just five years changed the story over the entire 20 year holding period, leading to significant outperformance by Berkshire.

Gold underperformed Berkshire financially over this period, but it also provided zero benefits for society. At the end of 1985, Berkshire employed 5,120 people through its wholly-owned subsidiaries. This does not count the number of employees at the many businesses that Berkshire partially owned. The equity invested in Berkshire funded this employment, as well as products and services that consumers demanded. As a society, we should be thankful for Berkshire's contributions.

176

Notes

I. The Preface

1. Carol J. Loomis, *Tap Dancing to Work* (New York: Penguin Group, 2012), 196.

II. The Prologue

1. Blue Chip Stamps, *1974 Annual Report*, 5.
2. Charles T. Munger's 1982 Letter to Blue Chip Stamps Shareholders, February 17, 1983.
3. *Moody's Industrial Manual.* (New York: Moody's Investors Service, Inc, 1965), 296.
4. https://archive.fortune.com/magazines/fortune/fortune500_archive/full/1965/
5. Berkshire Hathaway, *1965 Annual Report*, 8.
6. General Electric, *1965 Annual Report*, 30.
7. *Moody's Industrial Manual.* (New York: Moody's Investors Service, Inc, 1966), 92.
8. Warren Buffett's 2019 Letter to Berkshire Hathaway Shareholders, February 22, 2020.

III. The Textile Mill 1955 - 1962

1. Berkshire Hathaway, *1955 Annual Report*, 2.
2. Berkshire Hathaway, *1955 Annual Report*, 6.
3. Berkshire Hathaway, *1955 Annual Report*, 7.
4. Berkshire Hathaway, *1955 Annual Report*, 9.
5. Lowenstein, Roger. *Buffett: The Making of an American Capitalist.* (New York: Random House, 1995), 126.
6. Berkshire Hathaway, *1955 Annual Report*, 7.
7. Ibid.
8. Berkshire Hathaway, *1955-1961 Annual Reports.*
9. Ibid.

177

10. Ibid.

11. Ibid.

12. Ibid.

13. Berkshire Hathaway, *1957-1961 Annual Reports*.

14. Berkshire Hathaway, *1955 Annual Report*, 3.

15. *Moody's Industrial Manual*. (New York: Moody's Investors Service, Inc, 1960), 84.

16. Berkshire Hathaway, *1956 Annual Report*, 6-7.

17. *Moody's Industrial Manual*. (New York: Moody's Investors Service, Inc, 1960), 84.

IV. The Investment 1962 - 1965

1. Schroeder, Alice. *The Snowball: Warren Buffett and the Business of Life*. (New York: Bantam, 2008), 271.

2. Berkshire Hathaway, *1962 Annual Report*, 7.

3. Berkshire Hathaway, *1962 Annual Report*, 9.

4. Berkshire Hathaway, *1962 Annual Report*, 8.

5. Berkshire Hathaway, *1956-1962 Annual Reports*.

6. Direct quotes from the Letters to Shareholders of Warren Buffett and Charlie Munger were reprinted with their permission.

7. Schroeder, Alice. *The Snowball: Warren Buffett and the Business of Life*. (New York: Bantam, 2008), 272-273.

8. Berkshire Hathaway. (1966). Form 10-K 1965, 1.

9. Ibid.

10. Warren Buffett's Letter to Buffett Partnership, Ltd, January 20, 1966, 6.

V. The Transition 1965 - 1967

1. Berkshire Hathaway, *1965 Annual Report*, 8.

2. Berkshire Hathaway, *1965 Annual Report*, 3.

3. Berkshire Hathaway, *1964 Annual Report*, 8.

4. Ibid.

5. Ibid.

6. Berkshire Hathaway, *1962-1965 Annual Reports*.

178

7. Berkshire Hathaway, *1966 Annual Report*, 6.

8. Berkshire Hathaway, *1965 Annual Report*, 9.

9. Berkshire Hathaway, *1965 Annual Report*, 6.

10. Berkshire Hathaway, *1965 Annual Report*, 8.

11. Berkshire Hathaway, *1965 Annual Report*, 7.

12. Berkshire Hathaway, *1965 Annual Report*, 6.

13. Berkshire Hathaway. (1967). Form 10-K 1966, 6.

14. Berkshire Hathaway, *1965 Annual Report*, 4.

15. Berkshire Hathaway, *1964 Annual Report*, 7.

16. Berkshire Hathaway, *1965 Annual Report*, 7.

17. Berkshire Hathaway. (1967). Form 10-K 1966, 11.

18. Berkshire Hathaway. (1968). Form 10-K 1967, 15.

19. Warren Buffett's 1985 Letter to Berkshire Hathaway Shareholders, March 4, 1986.

20. Berkshire Hathaway. (2020). Form 10-K 2019, K-1.

21. Berkshire Hathaway. (2020). Form 10-K 2019, K-70.

22. Warren Buffett's 2019 Letter to Berkshire Hathaway Shareholders, February 22, 2020

23. Berkshire Hathaway, *1965 Annual Report*, 6.

24. Berkshire Hathaway. (1967). Form 10-K 1966, 6.

25. Berkshire Hathaway. (1968). Form 10-K 1967, 15.

26. Berkshire Hathaway, *1965-1967 Annual Report*s.

27. Berkshire Hathaway. (1968). Form 10-K 1967, 12.

28. *Moody's Industrial Manual.* (New York: Moody's Investors Service, Inc, 1968), 438.

29. Ibid.

30. Ibid.

31. *Moody's Industrial Manual.* (New York: Moody's Investors Service, Inc, 1969), 839.

32. Berkshire Hathaway. (1968). Form 10-K 1967, 9.

33. Berkshire Hathaway. Form 10-K 1965-1969.

34. *Moody's Industrial Manual.* (New York: Moody's Investors Service, Inc, 1968), 437-438.

35. Berkshire Hathaway. (1968). Form 10-K 1967, 8.

36. Berkshire Hathaway. (1967). Form 10-K 1966, 6.

37. Berkshire Hathaway. (1967). Form 10-K 1966, 11.

38. Berkshire Hathaway. (1969). Form 10-K 1968, 14.

39. Calculated by taking net sales of textile products minus cost of sales minus administrative and selling expenses for 1967 and 1968.

40. Berkshire Hathaway. Form 10-K 1967-1968.

VI.   The Acquisitions 1967 - 1969

1. *Moody's Bank & Finance Manual.* (New York: Moody's Investors Service, Inc, 1965), 1482.

2. Ibid.

3. *Moody's Bank & Finance Manual.* (New York: Moody's Investors Service, Inc, 1956).

4. Berkshire Hathaway, *1955 Annual Report*, 9.

5. Berkshire Hathaway, *1955 Annual Report*, 7.

6. *Moody's Bank & Finance Manual.* (New York: Moody's Investors Service, Inc, 1956).

7. *Moody's Bank & Finance Manual.* (New York: Moody's Investors Service, Inc, 1956, 1961, and 1966).

8. Ibid.

9. *Moody's Bank & Finance Manual.* (New York: Moody's Investors Service, Inc, 1966), 1475.

10. Damodaran, Aswath. New York University. January 5, 2019. http://pages.stern.nyu.edu/~adamodar/New_Home_Page/datafile/his tretSPX.html

11. Warren Buffett's 2017 Letter to Berkshire Hathaway Shareholders, February 24, 2018, 6.

12. *Moody's Bank & Finance Manual.* (New York: Moody's Investors Service, Inc, 1967), 1513.

13. Berkshire Hathaway. (1968). Form 10-K 1967, 31.

14. *Moody's Bank & Finance Manual.* (New York: Moody's Investors Service, Inc, 1967), 1513.

15. Based on $15,619,638 of float calculated by the author using the 1966 balance sheet.

16. Berkshire Hathaway. Form 10-K 1966-1967.

17. Berkshire Hathaway. (1968). Form 10-K 1967, 10.

18. Berkshire Hathaway. (1968). Form 10-K 1967, 17.

19. *Best's Insurance Reports. Fire and Casualty.* (Morristown, NJ: A.M. Best Co., 1965), ix.

20. *Moody's Bank & Finance Manual.* (New York: Moody's Investors Service, Inc, 1965), 1482.

21. https://www.naic.org/documents/web_market_share_property_casua lty.pdf?17

22. Berkshire Hathaway, *1968 Annual Report*, 4.

23. Berkshire Hathaway. (1970). Form 10-K 1969, 16.

24. Berkshire Hathaway. (1970). Form 10-K 1969, 7.

25. Berkshire Hathaway, *1972 Annual Report*, 5.

26. Warren Buffett's 1969 BPL Letter to Partners, December 26, 1969, 2.

27. Berkshire Hathaway. (1970). Form 10-K 1969, 7.

28. https://www.omaha.com/money/newspaperman-omaha-native-stanf ord-lipsey-had-ear-and-trust-of/article_29c72a99-fe97-572e-976b-a 2c8d794475d.html

29. Warren Buffett's 1973 Letter to Berkshire Hathaway Shareholders, March 29, 1974, 3.

30. Berkshire Hathaway. (1970). Form 10-K 1969, 43.

31. *Moody's Bank & Finance Manual.* (New York: Moody's Investors Service, Inc, 1961).

32. *Moody's Bank & Finance Manual.* (New York: Moody's Investors Service, Inc, 1965), 304.

33. *Moody's Bank & Finance Manual.* (New York: Moody's Investors Service, Inc, 1945), 173.

34. *Moody's Bank & Finance Manual.* (New York: Moody's Investors Service, Inc, 1948), 44.

35. *Moody's Bank & Finance Manual.* (New York: Moody's Investors Service, Inc, 1945), 173.

36. Berkshire Hathaway. (1970). Form 10-K 1969, 44.

37. https://www.usinflationcalculator.com/

38. Bank of America Corp. (2020). Form 10-K 2019, 22 and 90.

39. Cullen/Frost Bankers (2020). Form 10-K 2019, 5 and 71.

40. Wells Fargo and Company (2020). Form 10-K 2019, 6 and 123.

41. Wells Fargo Bank, *1968 Annual Report*.

42. Damodaran, Aswath. New York University. January 5, 2019. http://pages.stern.nyu.edu/~adamodar/New_Home_Page/datafile/his tretSPX.html

43. Berkshire Hathaway. (1971). Form 10-K 1970, 49.

44. Berkshire Hathaway. (1969). Form 10-K 1968, 7.

45. Berkshire Hathaway. (1969). Form 10-K 1968, 14.

46. Berkshire Hathaway. (1971). Form 10-K 1970, 12.

47. Berkshire Hathaway. (1970). Form 10-K 1969, 43.

48. Berkshire Hathaway. (1974). Form 10-K 1973, F-22.

49. Berkshire Hathaway. (1979). Form 10-K 1978, F-102.

50. Berkshire Hathaway. (1970). Form 10-K 1969, 43.

51. Berkshire Hathaway. (1979). Form 10-K 1978, F-102.

52. Warren Buffett's 1980 Letter to Berkshire Hathaway Shareholders, February 27, 1981.

53. Lowenstein, Roger. *Buffett: The Making of an American Capitalist.* (New York: Random House, 1995), 130.

54. Berkshire Hathaway, *1964 Annual Report*, 7.

55. *Moody's Industrial Manual.* (New York: Moody's Investors Service, Inc, 1970).

56. Berkshire Hathaway. (1969). Form 10-K 1968, 2.

57. Berkshire Hathaway, *1962 Annual Report*, 8.

58. Berkshire Hathaway. (1970). Form 10-K 1969, 8.

59. Berkshire Hathaway. Form 10-K 1965-1969.

60. Berkshire Hathaway, *1962 Annual Report*, 8.

61. Berkshire Hathaway. (1966). Form 10-K 1965, 6-7.

62. Berkshire Hathaway. (1970). Form 10-K 1969, 7-8.

63. *Moody's Industrial Manual.* (New York: Moody's Investors Service, Inc, 1970).

64. Berkshire Hathaway. (1970). Form 10-K 1969, 8.

VII.   The Expansion 1970's

1. Berkshire Hathaway. (1974). Form 10-K 1973, 7.

2. Berkshire Hathaway. (1966). Form 10-K 1965, 7.

3. Berkshire Hathaway. (1974). Form 10-K 1973, 1.

4. Ibid.

5. Berkshire Hathaway. (1968). Form 10-K 1967, 23 and 31.

6. Berkshire Hathaway. (1974). Form 10-K 1973, F-2.

7. Berkshire Hathaway. (1966). Form 10-K 1965, 6.

8. Berkshire Hathaway. (1971). Form 10-K 1970, 9.

9. Berkshire Hathaway. (1975). Form 10-K 1974, F-9 and F-10.

10. Berkshire Hathaway. (1966). Form 10-K 1965, 7.

11. Berkshire Hathaway. (1968). Form 10-K 1967, 12.

12. Berkshire Hathaway. (1970). Form 10-K 1969, 7.

13. Berkshire Hathaway. (1974). Form 10-K 1973, F-2.

14. Berkshire Hathaway. (1974). Form 10-K 1973, F-12.

15. Berkshire Hathaway. (1974). Form 10-K 1973, F-2.

16. The $17.8 million of earnings before interest and taxes in 1973 was calculated by taking the 'Earnings from insurance underwriting and manufacturing operations before applicable income taxes' and adding back interest expense, pretax realized investment gains, and the equity in earnings of unconsolidated subsidiaries.

17. Berkshire Hathaway. (1974). Form 10-K 1973, F-3.

18. Berkshire Hathaway, *1971 Annual Report*, 15.

19. *Best's Insurance Reports. Fire and Casualty.* (Morristown, NJ: A.M. Best Co., 1965), 536.

20. Warren Buffett's 1971 Letter to Berkshire Hathaway Shareholders, March 13, 1972, 2.

21. The price to sales ratio was calculated by taking the total purchase price divided by the combined premiums written in 1967 of both National Indemnity and National Fire & Marine.

22. Berkshire Hathaway, *1971 Annual Report*, 15.

23. Berkshire Hathaway. (1974). Form 10-K 1973, 1.

24. Berkshire Hathaway. (1974). Form 10-K 1973, 2.

25. Berkshire Hathaway. (1975). Form 10-K 1974, 2.

26. Ibid.

27. Ibid.

28. Berkshire Hathaway. (1975). Form 10-K 1974, 9.

29. Berkshire Hathaway. (1977). Form 10-K 1976, 6.

30. Berkshire Hathaway. (1977). Form 10-K 1976, 7.

31. Berkshire Hathaway. (1986). Form 10-K 1985, 24.

32. Berkshire Hathaway. (1977). Form 10-K 1976, 7.

33. Berkshire Hathaway. (1976). Form 10-K 1975, 7.

34. Berkshire Hathaway. (1971). Form 10-K 1970, 31.

35. Berkshire Hathaway. (1975). Form 10-K 1974, 2.

36. Berkshire Hathaway. (1977). Form 10-K 1976, 6.

37. Damodaran, Aswath. New York University. January 5, 2019. http://pages.stern.nyu.edu/~adamodar/New_Home_Page/datafile/his tretSPX.html

38. Berkshire Hathaway. (1974). Form 10-K 1973, 1.

39. Berkshire Hathaway, *1985 Annual Report*, 41.

40. Buffett, "The Security I like Best", *Commercial and Financial Chronicle*, December 6, 1951.

41. Warren Buffett's 1995 Letter to Berkshire Hathaway Shareholders, March 1, 1996.

42. GEICO, *1974 Annual Report*, 4.

43. GEICO, *1974 Annual Report*, 8 and 26.

44. Warren Buffett's 1995 Letter to Berkshire Hathaway Shareholders, March 1, 1996.

45. Lowenstein, Roger. *Buffett: The Making of an American Capitalist.* (New York: Random House, 1995), 118.

46. Warren Buffett's 2019 Letter to Berkshire Hathaway Shareholders, February 22, 2020.

47. *Best's Insurance Reports. Fire and Casualty.* (Morristown, NJ: A.M. Best Co., 1965), x.

48. *Best's Insurance Reports. Fire and Casualty.* (Morristown, NJ: A.M. Best Co., 1975), 394B and 40.

49. GEICO, *1974 Annual Report*, 8 and 38.

50. GEICO, *1974 Annual Report*, 6.

51. This was calculated by taking a 25.4% underwriting loss times leverage of 3.93. This would equal about 100% of equity.

52. GEICO, *1974 Annual Report*, 8.

53. Ibid.

54. GEICO, *1974 Annual Report*, 33.

55. GEICO, *1974 Annual Report*, 8.

56. GEICO, *1974 Annual Report*, 33.

57. GEICO, *1975 Annual Report*, 5.

58. GEICO, *1975 Annual Report*, 12.

59. GEICO, *1975 Annual Report*, 3.

60. GEICO, *1974 Annual Report*, 26.

61. GEICO, *1976 Annual Report*, 15.

62. GEICO, *1976 Annual Report*, 4.

63. GEICO, *1976 Annual Report*, 2.

64. GEICO, *1976 Annual Report*, 18.

65. GEICO, *1976 Annual Report*, 23.

66. GEICO, *1976 Annual Report*, 1.

67. Berkshire Hathaway. (1977). Form 10-K 1976, S-1.

68. GEICO, *1976 Annual Report*, 32.

69. Berkshire Hathaway. (1977). Form 10-K 1976, F-20.

70. Berkshire Hathaway. (1977). Form 10-K 1976, 6.

71. GEICO, *1976 Annual Report*, 22.

72. Berkshire Hathaway. (1981). Form 10-K 1980, 40.

73. Warren Buffett's 1979 Letter to Berkshire Hathaway Shareholders, March 3, 1980.

74. GEICO, *1980 Annual Report*, 23.

75. Warren Buffett's 1980 Letter to Berkshire Hathaway Shareholders, February 27, 1981.

76. Ibid.

77. Warren Buffett's 1985 Letter to Berkshire Hathaway Shareholders, March 4, 1986.

78. GEICO, *1980 Annual Report*, 16.

79. GEICO, *1984 Annual Report*, 2.

80. GEICO, *1980 Annual Report*, 16.

81. *Reminiscences of Abraham Lincoln by distinguished men of his time / collected and edited by Allen Thorndike Rice.* (1853-1889). New York: Harper & Brothers Publishers, 1909. https://quod.lib.umich.edu/l/lincoln2/BCC9571.0001.001/262?rgn=full+text;view=image

82. GEICO, *1976 Annual Report*, 6.

83. GEICO, *1976 Annual Report*, 22.

84. GEICO, *1977 Annual Report*, 4.

85. Lowenstein, Roger. *Buffett: The Making of an American Capitalist.* (New York: Random House, 1995), 198.

86. Lowenstein, Roger. *Buffett: The Making of an American Capitalist.* (New York: Random House, 1995), 199.
87. Berkshire Hathaway, *1977 Annual Report*, 19.
88. Berkshire Hathaway. (1978). Form 10-K 1977, 2.
89. Berkshire Hathaway, *1977 Annual Report*, 19.
90. Berkshire Hathaway. (1978). Form 10-K 1977, 17.
91. Berkshire Hathaway. (1976). Form 10-K 1975, F-6.
92. Berkshire Hathaway. (1976). Form 10-K 1975, F-2.
93. Berkshire Hathaway. (1976). Form 10-K 1975, F-7.
94. Berkshire Hathaway. (1977). Form 10-K 1976, 9.
95. Berkshire Hathaway. (1977). Form 10-K 1976, 2.
96. Berkshire Hathaway. (1977). Form 10-K 1976, 9.
97. Berkshire Hathaway. (1977). Form 10-K 1976, F-3.
98. Berkshire Hathaway. (1977). Form 10-K 1976, 2.
99. Berkshire Hathaway. (1978). Form 10-K 1977, 20.

VIII.   The Other Companies

1. *Moody's Industrial Manual.* (New York: Moody's Investors Service, Inc, 1968), 524.
2. Ibid.
3. Schroeder, Alice. *The Snowball: Warren Buffett and the Business of Life.* (New York: Bantam, 2008), 293.
4. *Moody's Industrial Manual.* (New York: Moody's Investors Service, Inc, 1968), 524.
5. Ibid.
6. *Moody's Industrial Manual.* (New York: Moody's Investors Service, Inc, 1969), 1878.
7. Warren Buffett's 1968 BPL Letter to Partners, January 22, 1969, 4.
8. Warren Buffett's 1978 Letter to Berkshire Hathaway Shareholders, March 26, 1979.
9. Warren Buffett's 1969 BPL Letter to Partners, December 5, 1969, 1.
10. Berkshire Hathaway. (1979). Form 10-K 1978, 20.

11. Warren Buffett's 1969 BPL Letter to Partners, December 5, 1969, 1.

12. Blue Chip Stamps, *1969 Annual Report*, 4.

13. Ibid.

14. Ibid.

15. Ibid.

16. Kaufman, Peter. *Poor Charlie's Almanack.* (PCA Publications, L.L.C., 2008), Chronology.

17. Blue Chip Stamps, *1969 Annual Report*, 1.

18. Blue Chip Stamps. (1980). Form 10-K 1979,8.

19. Blue Chip Stamps, *1969 Annual Report*, 5.

20. Ibid.

21. Blue Chip Stamps, *1974 Annual Report*, 4-5.

22. *Moody's OTC Industrial Manual.* (New York: Moody's Investors Service, Inc, 1970), 465.

23. *Moody's Industrial Manual.* (New York: Moody's Investors Service, Inc, 1972), 2098.

24. *Moody's Industrial Manual.* (New York: Moody's Investors Service, Inc, 1973), 582.

25. *Moody's Industrial Manual.* (New York: Moody's Investors Service, Inc, 1972), 2098-2099.

26. *Moody's Industrial Manual.* (New York: Moody's Investors Service, Inc, 1960-1972).

27. Ibid.

28. Damodaran, Aswath. New York University. January 5, 2019. http://pages.stern.nyu.edu/~adamodar/New_Home_Page/datafile/his tretSPX.html

29. *Moody's Industrial Manual.* (New York: Moody's Investors Service, Inc, 1960-1972).

30. *Moody's OTC Industrial Manual.* (New York: Moody's Investors Service, Inc, 1972), 769.

31. Ibid.

32. *Moody's Industrial Manual.* (New York: Moody's Investors Service, Inc, 1972), 2099.

33. Warren Buffett's 1983 Letter to Berkshire Hathaway Shareholders, March 14, 1984, 16.

34. Warren Buffett's 1984 Letter to Berkshire Hathaway Shareholders, February 25, 1985, 6.

35. See's Candies. *See's Candies Timeline.* https://www.sees.com/timeline/

36. Dianne de Guzman and Alix Martichoux, *Inside See's Candies South San Francisco factory: See how they craft chocolates by hand*, SF Gate, November 16, 2017. https://www.sfgate.com/food/article/Made-Bay-Area-See-s-Candy-S outh-San-Francisco-12339742.php

37. Light, Murray. *From Butler to Buffett: The Story Behind the Buffalo News.* (New York: Prometheus Books, 2004), 197.

38. Light, Murray. *From Butler to Buffett: The Story Behind the Buffalo News.* (New York: Prometheus Books, 2004), 211.

39. Light, Murray. *From Butler to Buffett: The Story Behind the Buffalo News.* (New York: Prometheus Books, 2004), 30.

40. Light, Murray. *From Butler to Buffett: The Story Behind the Buffalo News.* (New York: Prometheus Books, 2004), 33.

41. Schroeder, Alice. *The Snowball: Warren Buffett and the Business of Life.* (New York: Bantam, 2008), 463.

42. Blue Chip Stamps, *1978 Annual Report*, 12.

43. Blue Chip Stamps, *1978 Annual Report*, 14.

44. Light, Murray. *From Butler to Buffett: The Story Behind the Buffalo News.* (New York: Prometheus Books, 2004), 231.

45. Light, Murray. *From Butler to Buffett: The Story Behind the Buffalo News.* (New York: Prometheus Books, 2004), 191-192.

46. Schroeder, Alice. *The Snowball: Warren Buffett and the Business of Life.* (New York: Bantam, 2008), 464.

47. Light, Murray. *From Butler to Buffett: The Story Behind the Buffalo News.* (New York: Prometheus Books, 2004), 211.

48. Light, Murray. *From Butler to Buffett: The Story Behind the Buffalo News.* (New York: Prometheus Books, 2004), 220.

49. Blue Chip Stamps, *1978 Annual Report*, 5.

50. Warren Buffett's 1989 Letter to Berkshire Hathaway Shareholders, March 2, 1990.

51. Warren Buffett's 1982 Letter to Berkshire Hathaway Shareholders, March 3, 1983.

52. Berkshire Hathaway, *1985 Annual Report*, 39 and 49.

53. *Moody's OTC Industrial Manual.* (New York: Moody's Investors Service, Inc, 1977), 844.

54. Pinkerton's, *1972 Annual Report*, 16.

55. *Moody's OTC Industrial Manual.* (New York: Moody's Investors Service, Inc, 1968), 811.

56. *Moody's OTC Industrial Manual.* (New York: Moody's Investors Service, Inc, 1977), 511.

57. *Moody's OTC Industrial Manual.* (New York: Moody's Investors Service, Inc, 1975), 8060.

58. *Moody's OTC Industrial Manual.* (New York: Moody's Investors Service, Inc, 1972), 2885.

59. *Moody's OTC Industrial Manual.* (New York: Moody's Investors Service, Inc, 1975), 8060.

60. Damodaran, Aswath. New York University. January 5, 2019. http://pages.stern.nyu.edu/~adamodar/New_Home_Page/datafile/his tretSPX.html

61.Blue Chip Stamps, *1979 Annual Report*, Schedule I.

62. Blue Chip Stamps, *1978 Annual Report*, 12.

63. *Moody's OTC Industrial Manual.* (New York: Moody's Investors Service, Inc, 1977), 511.

64. Lewin, Tamar. *PINKERTON'S IS BEING ACQUIRED.* The New York Times: December 8, 1982. https://www.nytimes.com/1982/12/08/business/pinkerton-s-is-being-acquired.html

65. Charles T. Munger to Blue Chip Stamps shareholders year-end 1982, February 17, 1983.

66. *Moody's OTC Industrial Manual.* (New York: Moody's Investors Service, Inc, 1979-1982).

67. Schroeder, Alice. *The Snowball: Warren Buffett and the Business of Life.* (New York: Bantam, 2008), 883.

68. *Moody's Bank & Finance Manual.* (New York: Moody's Investors Service, Inc, 1975), 1178.

69. *Moody's Bank & Finance Manual.* (New York: Moody's Investors Service, Inc, 1972), 1666.

70. Damodaran, Aswath. New York University. January 5, 2019.

http://pages.stern.nyu.edu/~adamodar/New_Home_Page/datafile/his
tretSPX.html

71. *Moody's OTC Industrial Manual.* (New York: Moody's Investors Service, Inc, 1975), 275.

72. *Moody's OTC Industrial Manual.* (New York: Moody's Investors Service, Inc, 1977), 844.

73. *Moody's Bank & Finance Manual.* (New York: Moody's Investors Service, Inc, 1975), 1178.

74. Wesco Financial. (1979). Form 10-K 1978, 13.

75. *Moody's Bank & Finance Manual.* (New York: Moody's Investors Service, Inc, 1975), 1178.

76. Wesco Financial. (1979). Form 10-K 1978, 13.

77. Wesco Financial. (1981). Form 10-K 1980, F-24.

78. *Moody's Bank & Finance Manual.* (New York: Moody's Investors Service, Inc, 1982), 2333.

79. *Moody's Bank & Finance Manual.* (New York: Moody's Investors Service, Inc, 1985), 2449.

80. *Moody's Bank & Finance Manual.* (New York: Moody's Investors Service, Inc, 1987), 2764.

81. *Moody's Bank & Finance Manual.* (New York: Moody's Investors Service, Inc, 1985), 2449.

82. Charles T. Munger to Wesco shareholders year-end 1985, February 13, 1986.

83. *Moody's Bank & Finance Manual.* (New York: Moody's Investors Service, Inc, 1985), 2449.

84. *Moody's Bank & Finance Manual.* (New York: Moody's Investors Service, Inc, 1987), 2764.

85. General Foods Corporation, *1985 Annual Report*, 17.

86. Warren Buffett's 1980 Letter to Berkshire Hathaway Shareholders, February 27, 1981.

87. Warren Buffett's 1983 Letter to Berkshire Hathaway Shareholders, March 14, 1983.

88. Berkshire Hathaway. (1984). Form 10-K 1983, 20.

89. General Foods Corporation, *1975 Annual Report*, 20.

90. General Foods Corporation, *1979 Annual Report*, 31.

91. General Foods Corporation, *1985 Annual Report*, 30.

92. Warren Buffett's 1984 Letter to Berkshire Hathaway Shareholders, February 25, 1985.

93. Cole, Robert. *PHILIP MORRIS TO BUY GENERAL FOODS FOR $5.8 BILLION.* The New York Times. September 28, 1985. https://www.nytimes.com/1985/09/28/business/philip-morris-to-buy-general-foods-for-5.8-billion.html

94. Berkshire Hathaway, *1985 Annual Report*, 37.

95. Charles T. Munger to Wesco shareholders year-end 1985, February 13, 1986.

96. *Moody's Bank & Finance Manual.* (New York: Moody's Investors Service, Inc, 1987), 2764.

97. Berkshire Hathaway, *1985 Annual Report*, 25.

98. *Moody's Public Utilities Manual.* (John Moody, 1929), 2185.

99. Lowenstein, Roger. *Buffett: The Making of an American Capitalist.* (New York: Random House, 1995), 213.

100. Sloan, Allan. *The Battle to Buy a Bridge.* The New York Times. January 1, 1978. https://www.nytimes.com/1978/01/01/archives/the-battle-to-buy-a-bridge-the-battle-to-buy-a-bridge.html

101. *Moody's Transportation Manual.* (New York: Moody's Investors Service, Inc., 1977), 1529.

102. *Moody's Transportation Manual.* (New York: Moody's Investors Service, Inc., 1970-1979).

103. Sloan, Allan. *The Battle to Buy a Bridge.* The New York Times. January 1, 1978. https://www.nytimes.com/1978/01/01/archives/the-battle-to-buy-a-bridge-the-battle-to-buy-a-bridge.html

104. *Moody's Transportation Manual.* (New York: Moody's Investors Service, Inc., 1977), 1529.

105. Ibid.

106. Damodaran, Aswath. New York University. January 5, 2019. http://pages.stern.nyu.edu/~adamodar/New_Home_Page/datafile/histretSPX.html

107. Berkshire Hathaway. (1975). Form 10-K 1974, S-2.

108. Wesco Financial. (1979). Form 10-K 1978, 7.

109. Sloan, Allan. *The Battle to Buy a Bridge.* The New York

Times. January 1, 1978.
https://www.nytimes.com/1978/01/01/archives/the-battle-to-buy-a-b
ridge-the-battle-to-buy-a-bridge.html

110. Wesco Financial. (1979). Form 10-K 1978, 7.

111. Wesco Financial, *1978 Annual Report*, 1.

112. Ibid.

113. Blue Chip Stamps, *1979 Annual Report*, 9.

114. *Moody's Bank & Finance Manual.* (New York: Moody's Investors Service, Inc., 1982), 2333.

115. Ibid.

116. Ibid.

117. *Moody's Bank & Finance Manual.* (New York: Moody's Investors Service, Inc., 1987), 2764.

118. Berkshire Hathaway. (1973). Form 10-K 1972, S-9.

119. *Moody's OTC Industrial Manual.* (New York: Moody's Investors Service, Inc., 1972), 770.

120. Berkshire Hathaway, *1972 Annual Report*, 16.

121. Warren Buffett's 1977 Letter to Berkshire Hathaway Shareholders, March 14, 1978.

122. Warren Buffett's 1978 Letter to Berkshire Hathaway Shareholders, March 26, 1979.

123. *Moody's OTC Industrial Manual.* (New York: Moody's Investors Service, Inc., 1970), 465.

124. *Moody's OTC Industrial Manual.* (New York: Moody's Investors Service, Inc., 1971), 716.

125. Blue Chip Stamps, *1974 Annual Report*, 5.

126. Blue Chip Stamps, *1974 Annual Report*, 7.

127. *Moody's OTC Industrial Manual.* (New York: Moody's Investors Service, Inc., 1972), 770.

128. Blue Chip Stamps, *1974 Annual Report*, 6-7.

129. Blue Chip Stamps, *1979 Annual Report*, 10.

130. Blue Chip Stamps, *1979 Annual Report*, 9.

131. Blue Chip Stamps, *1974 Annual Report*, 8.

132. Blue Chip Stamps, *1978 Annual Report*, 12.

133. Blue Chip Stamps, *1974 Annual Report*, 4.

134. *Moody's OTC Industrial Manual.* (New York: Moody's

Investors Service, Inc., 1975), 276.

135. Ibid.

136. Blue Chip Stamps, *1974 Annual Report*, 8.

137. *Moody's OTC Industrial Manual.* (New York: Moody's Investors Service, Inc., 1975), 276.

138. Blue Chip Stamps, *1974 Annual Report*, 7.

139. Damodaran, Aswath. New York University. January 5, 2019. http://pages.stern.nyu.edu/~adamodar/New_Home_Page/datafile/his tretSPX.html

140. Blue Chip Stamps, *1974 Annual Report*, 7.

141. Blue Chip Stamps, *1974 Annual Report*, 6-7.

142. Berkshire Hathaway. (1975). Form 10-K 1974, F-19.

143. Berkshire Hathaway. (1973). Form 10-K 1972, S-9.

144. Berkshire Hathaway. (1975). Form 10-K 1974, F-19.

145. Blue Chip Stamps, *1974 Annual Report*, 11.

146. Blue Chip Stamps, *1974 Annual Report*, 7.

147. Blue Chip Stamps, *1980 Annual Report*, 16.

148. Blue Chip Stamps, *1980 Annual Report*, 15.

149. Blue Chip Stamps, *1980 Annual Report*, 28.

150. Ibid.

151. Damodaran, Aswath. New York University. January 5, 2019. http://pages.stern.nyu.edu/~adamodar/New_Home_Page/datafile/his tretSPX.html

152. Blue Chip Stamps, *1980 Annual Report*, 20.

153. Lowe, Janet. *Damn Right! Behind the Scenes with Berkshire Hathaway Billionaire Charlie Munger..* (New York: John Wiley & Sons, Inc. 2000), 118.

154. Berkshire Hathaway, *1984 Annual Report*, 64.

IX.   The Conglomerate

1. Berkshire Hathaway. (1970). Form 10-K 1969, 25 and 34.

2. Berkshire Hathaway. (1973). Form 10-K 1972, 12.

3. Berkshire Hathaway. (1970). Form 10-K 1969, 26 and 35.

4. Berkshire Hathaway. (1973). Form 10-K 1972, 13.

5. Berkshire Hathaway. (1974). Form 10-K 1973, F-4.

6. Berkshire Hathaway. (1972). Form 10-K 1971, 13.

7. Berkshire Hathaway. (1973). Form 10-K 1972, 13.

8. Berkshire Hathaway. (1970). Form 10-K 1969, 25 and 34.

9. Berkshire Hathaway. (1980). Form 10-K 1979, F-6.

10. Warren Buffett's 1990 Letter to Berkshire Hathaway Shareholders, March 1, 1991.

11. Berkshire Hathaway. (1976). Form 10-K 1975, 5.

12. Berkshire Hathaway. (1976). Form 10-K 1975, 7.

13. Berkshire Hathaway. (1980). Form 10-K 1979, F-12.

14. Berkshire Hathaway. (1976). Form 10-K 1975, 5.

15. Ibid.

16. Ibid.

17. Schroeder, Alice. *The Snowball: Warren Buffett and the Business of Life.* (New York: Bantam, 2008), 420.

18. Ibid.

19. Berkshire Hathaway. (1970). Form 10-K 1969, 7-8.

20. Berkshire Hathaway. (1975). Form 10-K 1974, F-2 and F-3.

21. Berkshire Hathaway. (1973). Form 10-K 1972, S-9.

22. Ibid.

23. Berkshire Hathaway. (1974). Form 10-K 1973, S-3 and S-5.

24. Berkshire Hathaway. (1975). Form 10-K 1974, F-19 and S-3.

25. Damodaran, Aswath. New York University. January 5, 2019. http://pages.stern.nyu.edu/~adamodar/New_Home_Page/datafile/his tretSPX.html

26. Berkshire Hathaway. (1975). Form 10-K 1974, S-2.

27. Berkshire Hathaway. (1975). Form 10-K 1974, S-3.

28. Berkshire Hathaway. (1975). Form 10-K 1974, F-19.

29. Charlie Munger, BBC Interview. https://www.youtube.com/watch?v=3WkpQ4PpId4&feature=emb_ti tle

30. The Washington Post Company, *1971 Annual Report*, 1.

31. Ibid.

32. Graham, Katharine. *Personal History.* (New York: Random House, 1997), 442 and 451.

33. Graham, Katharine. *Personal History.* (New York: Random House, 1997), 494.

34. Damodaran, Aswath. New York University. January 5, 2019. http://pages.stern.nyu.edu/~adamodar/New_Home_Page/datafile/histretSPX.html

35. The Washington Post Company, *1971 Annual Report*, 25.

36. The Washington Post Company, *1971 Annual Report*, 23 and 25.

37. The Washington Post Company, *1973 Annual Report*, 9.

38. The Washington Post Company, *1973 Annual Report*, 10.

39. The Washington Post Company. (1975). Form 10-K 1974, 1.

40. The Washington Post Company. (1975). Form 10-K 1974, 2.

41. Berkshire Hathaway. (1974). Form 10-K 1973, S-3.

42. The Washington Post Company, *1973 Annual Report*, 9.

43. The Washington Post Company, *1973 Annual Report*, 10.

44. The Washington Post Company, *1973 Annual Report*, 1.

45. Damodaran, Aswath. New York University. January 5, 2019. http://pages.stern.nyu.edu/~adamodar/New_Home_Page/datafile/histretSPX.html

46. The Washington Post Company, *1973 Annual Report*, 10.

47. The Washington Post Company, *1983 Annual Report*, 39.

48. The Washington Post Company, *1983 Annual Report*, 49.

49. The Washington Post Company, *1974 Annual Report*, 1.

50. The Washington Post Company, *1978 Annual Report*, 2.

51. The Washington Post Company, *1984 Annual Report*, 7.

52. The Washington Post Company, *1973 Annual Report*, 9.

53. The Washington Post Company, *1985 Annual Report*, 35.

54. Warren Buffett's 1985 Letter to Berkshire Hathaway Shareholders, March 4, 1986.

55. Ibid.

56. Berkshire Hathaway, *1985 Annual Report*, 25.

57. Berkshire Hathaway. (1984). Form 10-K 1983, 23.

58. Warren Buffett's 1983 Letter to Berkshire Hathaway Shareholders, March 14, 1984.

59. Warren Buffett's 1984 Letter to Berkshire Hathaway Shareholders, February 25, 1985.

60. Berkshire Hathaway. (1984). Form 10-K 1983, 20.

61. Warren Buffett's 1984 Letter to Berkshire Hathaway Shareholders, February 25, 1985.

62. Ibid.

63. Warren Buffett's 1984 Letter to Berkshire Hathaway Shareholders, February 25, 1985.

64. Ibid.

65. Wal-Mart, *1984 Annual Report*, 16.

66. Berkshire Hathaway. (1979). Form 10-K 1978, 1.

67. Ibid.

68. Berkshire Hathaway. (1979). Form 10-K 1978, 31.

69. Berkshire Hathaway. (1968). Form 10-K 1967, 23 and 31.

70. Berkshire Hathaway. (1979). Form 10-K 1978, F-3.

71. Berkshire Hathaway, *1984 Annual Report*, 25.

72. Berkshire Hathaway, *1984 Annual Report*, 24.

73. Berkshire Hathaway. (1980). Form 10-K 1979, F-12.

74. Berkshire Hathaway, *1979 Annual Report*, 12.

75. Berkshire Hathaway, *1979 Annual Report*, 24.

76. Berkshire Hathaway. (1981). Form 10-K 1980, 40.

77. Berkshire Hathaway, *1984 Annual Report*, 41.

78. Berkshire Hathaway. (1981). Form 10-K 1980, 21.

79. Berkshire Hathaway, *1985 Annual Report*, 25.

80. Berkshire Hathaway, *1985 Annual Report*, 31.

81. Berkshire Hathaway. (1981). Form 10-K 1980, 21 and 30.

82. Berkshire Hathaway, *1985 Annual Report*, 25 and 33.

X.   The Conclusion

1. Berkshire Hathaway. (1971). Form 10-K 1970, 9.

2. Berkshire Hathaway. (1979). Form 10-K 1978, F-2.

3. Warren Buffett's 1978 Letter to Berkshire Hathaway Shareholders, March 26, 1979.

4. Warren Buffett's 1985 Letter to Berkshire Hathaway Shareholders, March 4, 1986.

5. Warren Buffett's 1978 Letter to Berkshire Hathaway Shareholders, March 26, 1979.

6. Schroeder, Alice. *The Snowball: Warren Buffett and the Business of Life.* (New York: Bantam, 2008), 271.

7. Warren Buffett's Letter to Buffett Partnership, Ltd, January 20,

1966, 6.

8. Berkshire Hathaway. (1966). Form 10-K 1965, 1.

9. Berkshire Hathaway. (1968). Form 10-K 1967, 1.

10. Berkshire Hathaway, *1985 Annual Report*, 70.

11. Lowenstein, Roger. *Buffett: The Making of an American Capitalist.* (New York: Random House, 1995), 114.

12. Lowenstein, Roger. *Buffett: The Making of an American Capitalist.* (New York: Random House, 1995), 93.

13. Warren Buffett's 1994 Letter to Berkshire Hathaway Shareholders, March 7, 1995.

14. Ibid.

15. Berkshire Hathaway. (1968). Form 10-K 1967, 15.

16. *Moody's Bank & Finance Manual.* (New York: Moody's Investors Service, Inc, 1968), 1553.

17. Ibid.

18. Berkshire Hathaway. (1969). Form 10-K 1968, 14.

19. Berkshire Hathaway. (1968). Form 10-K 1967, 12.

20. *Moody's Industrial Manual.* (New York: Moody's Investors Service, Inc, 1968), 438.

21. Grossman, Peter. *American Express: The Unofficial History of the People Who Built the Great Financial Empire.* (New York: Crown Publishers, Inc., 1987), 84.

22. Grossman, Peter. *American Express: The Unofficial History of the People Who Built the Great Financial Empire.* (New York: Crown Publishers, Inc., 1987), 93.

23. Grossman, Peter. *American Express: The Unofficial History of the People Who Built the Great Financial Empire.* (New York: Crown Publishers, Inc., 1987), 280.

24. American Express, *1965 Annual Report*, 10.

25. Ibid.

26. Grossman, Peter. *American Express: The Unofficial History of the People Who Built the Great Financial Empire.* (New York: Crown Publishers, Inc., 1987), 239.

27. American Express, *1965 Annual Report*, 29.

28. *Moody's Bank & Finance Manual.* (New York: Moody's Investors Service, Inc, 1956), 848.

29. Damodaran, Aswath. New York University. January 5, 2019. http://pages.stern.nyu.edu/~adamodar/New_Home_Page/datafile/his tretSPX.html

30. Grossman, Peter. *American Express: The Unofficial History of the People Who Built the Great Financial Empire.* (New York: Crown Publishers, Inc., 1987), 7 and 207.

31. American Express, *1962 Annual Report*, 2.

32. American Express, *1961 Annual Report*, 11.

33. Grossman, Peter. *American Express: The Unofficial History of the People Who Built the Great Financial Empire.* (New York: Crown Publishers, Inc., 1987), 303.

34. Grossman, Peter. *American Express: The Unofficial History of the People Who Built the Great Financial Empire.* (New York: Crown Publishers, Inc., 1987), 6.

35. Grossman, Peter. *American Express: The Unofficial History of the People Who Built the Great Financial Empire.* (New York: Crown Publishers, Inc., 1987), 94.

36. American Express, *1965 Annual Report*, 29.

37. Ibid.

38. *Moody's Bank & Finance Manual.* (New York: Moody's Investors Service, Inc, 1966), 1475.

39. Berkshire Hathaway. (1974). Form 10-K 1973, F-15.

40. American Express, *1965 Annual Report*, 29.

41. Berkshire Hathaway. (1969). Form 10-K 1968, 14.

42. Berkshire Hathaway, *1985 Annual Report*, 70.

43. Damodaran, Aswath. New York University. January 5, 2019. http://pages.stern.nyu.edu/~adamodar/New_Home_Page/datafile/his tretSPX.html

44. Berkshire Hathaway, *1985 Annual Report*, 25 and 70.

45. Berkshire Hathaway, *1964 Annual Report*, 11.

46. Berkshire Hathaway. (1968). Form 10-K 1967, 7.

47. Berkshire Hathaway, *1985 Annual Report*, 25.

48. Berkshire Hathaway. (1975). Form 10-K 1974, 20.

49. Berkshire Hathaway. (1983). Form 10-K 1982, 13.

50. Berkshire Hathaway. (1971). Form 10-K 1970, 2.

51. Carol J. Loomis, *Tap Dancing to Work* (New York: Penguin

Group, 2012), 255.

52. Berkshire Hathaway. (2006). Schedule 14A Definitive Proxy Statement. March 13, 2006.

53. Ibid.

54. Berkshire Hathaway. (1972). Form 10-K 1971, 5 and 13.

55. Berkshire Hathaway. (1985). Form 10-K 1984, 24-25.

56. American International Group, Inc., *1984 Annual Report*, 41.

57. Berkshire Hathaway. (1979). Form 10-K 1978, F-2.

58. Berkshire Hathaway, *1985 Annual Report*, 25.

59. https://archive.fortune.com/magazines/fortune/fortune500_archive/full/1965/

60. Damodaran, Aswath. New York University. January 5, 2019. http://pages.stern.nyu.edu/~adamodar/New_Home_Page/datafile/histretSPX.html

61. Ibid.

62. https://www.minneapolisfed.org/about-us/monetary-policy/inflation-calculator/consumer-price-index-1913-

63. Damodaran, Aswath. New York University. January 5, 2019. http://pages.stern.nyu.edu/~adamodar/New_Home_Page/datafile/histretSPX.html

64. https://www.minneapolisfed.org/about-us/monetary-policy/inflation-calculator/consumer-price-index-1913-

Made in the USA
Middletown, DE
21 July 2020